THE
VAMPIRE
CINEMA

THE VAMPIRE CINEMA

by David Pirie

'Her smile and her small pointed teeth
reminded me of one of those old vampire films
they used to show in the cinerama museums.'

(Jean-Luc Godard: *Alphaville*)

Galley Press

A QUARTO BOOK

Published in this edition by Galley Press,
an imprint of W. H. Smith and Son Limited,
Registered No 237811 England. Trading as
WHS Distributors, St John's House,
East Street, Leicester, LE1 6NE

ISBN 0 86136 793 6

First published 1977

This book was designed and produced by
Quarto Publishing Limited
32 Kingly Court, London W1
Art Editor: Roger Daniels

Phototypeset in England by
Filmtype Services Limited, Scarborough

Reprinted 1984
by Leefung-Asco Printers Limited,
Hong Kong

Frontispiece and Contents: A scene from Jean Rollin's *Requiem pour un Vampire.*
Endpapers: Christopher Lee in *Dracula Prince of Darkness.*

CONTENTS

Note: all chapter title quotations are taken from Bram Stoker's *Dracula*.

INTRODUCTION

It would be hard to imagine a supernatural and religious concept more appropriate to the second half of the 20th century than the vampire. In the context of waning spiritual convictions, vampirism remains the most physical, the least spiritual of all supernatural manifestations. It records the triumph of sex over death, of flesh over spirit, of the corporeal over the invisible. It denies almost everything other than the gratification of the senses by physical means. It is the most materialistic of all possible cosmologies.

And it is precisely this palpable, three-dimensional quality that has made the vampire so promising and lucrative a subject for film-makers. Ghosts, werewolves, poltergeists and most other apparitions can be unsatisfactory, and sometimes derisory, on the screen. They are more easily handled in literature. But the vampire feeds on the very stuff of wish-fulfilment and dream which is at the essence of the cinematic experience. He or she is the focus of all our most graphic and repressed fantasies. In this respect the vampire is not far removed from the giant fantasy figures presented by the film companies as 'stars'.

Until the late 1950s, vampirism was – in production ratio terms – simply a minor movie theme. Indeed, until that time even the most intrepid and meticulous researcher would have been hard pressed to come up with any more than two dozen titles. There was the great cycle from Universal Studios in Hollywood, inaugurated by Bela Lugosi in the 1931 *Dracula*. And beyond that only a few isolated films made by different producers at different times. Then, from 1957, for a period of about fifteen years from at least ten countries (America, England, Italy, Spain, Mexico, France, Belgium, Germany, Japan and the Philippines) it is possible to count around two hundred vampire movies of every conceivable kind: from the polished Gothic melodramas of Hammer to the Baroque extravagance of the Mexican *Nostradamus* series; from the fleshy humour of Warhol and Morrissey to the ascetic seriousness of avant-garde enthusiasts like the Spanish film-maker Pedro Portabella.

The range of these films both in tone and content is much wider than a glance at the more familiar titles might suggest. They reflect the concerns and styles of completely different cultures and in some cases completely different approaches to film production: Poverty Row quickies rub shoulders with productions of little commercial ambition (Lommel's *Tenderness of the Wolves* for example). But the overwhelming majority of vampire pictures were definitely at the lower end of the commercial spectrum, produced with the intention of making a rapid profit, usually on short schedules and with a minimum of resources.

It is for this reason that in the early seventies the flood of these films showed signs of evaporating almost as quickly as it had begun. The word had presumably gone out around the end of 1973 that the vampire was no longer guaranteed box-office. A very rough tally suggests that in 1974 the international production of vampire movies fell to something like a sixth of the previous year's total. And since then it has been no more than a trickle largely sustained by those Latin countries like Mexico which fall less in line with international box-office trends and also (this may be even more significant) persist in censoring sex on the screen.

There would seem to be strong grounds for linking the commercial decline in vampire movies with the recent mushrooming of hardcore and softcore sexploitation. There has never been any question that the primary appeal of the films lay in their latent erotic content. And by a peculiar irony the freedom from censorship restrictions that enabled film-makers to tackle the visually graphic subject of vampires in the first place has now – in the mid-seventies – enabled them to move on to even more explicit erotic material. It remains to be seen whether the graphic portrayal of sexuality on the screen can ever finally have the same suggestive power as the oral-sadistic metaphor it replaces, but that will be a fascinating subject for the film historians of the 1980s and 1990s.

In the meantime it is perhaps possible for us for the first time to chart the passage of the

CHRISTOPHER LEE

BERNARD MENEZ

MARIE-HELENE BREILLAT
dans

DRACULA PERE ET FILS

Une réalisation
GAUMONT-INTERNATIONAL
PRODUCTION 2000

Christopher Lee's final bow? The vampire film finally comes round to self-parody in *Dracula Père et Fils*, an irreverent French comedy on the degeneration of Dracula's line.

A long way from the dream-like quality of most vampire films is Lommel's gruesome account of the notorious Fritz Haarmann, *Tenderness of the Wolves*.

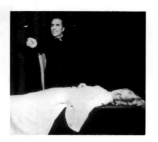

Udo Kier as the comic
Count Dracula in
search of virgin's blood
in Andy Warhol's
Blood for Dracula.

The last Hammer
Dracula: Christopher
Lee attempts to destroy
the world in *The
Satanic Rites of
Dracula.*

movie vampire with something like a sense of historical completeness. There will undoubtedly be more films but the sense of an epidemic has utterly vanished. The films of 1973 themselves look like a last desperate milking of overworked themes: in *The Satanic Rites of Dracula*, Hammer's last Dracula film to date, the Count was reduced ingeniously (but with more than a hint of desperation) to a London property speculator; the same year saw an atrocity called *Vampira* in which David Niven plays a modern comic Dracula being interviewed by *Playboy*.

No doubt I will be reminded that this kind of decadence is not new to the vampire movie. Universal, the original great horror studio, rode the form into the ground in the forties with films like *Abbott and Costello Meet Frankenstein*, which featured Dracula, Frankenstein and the Wolfman in a plot designed to squeeze the last drop of commercial life from Universal's original monster cycle. The vampire movie was pronounced dead then, and came back with a vengeance. But the circumstances are different now. With the vast backlog of vampire movies still readily available both in the cinema and on television, and with explicit sex movies dominating the pulp market, it is really necessary to imagine some drastic cultural reversal in order to envisage a return of the vampire's mass popularity.

The form will, however, always be popular with lovers of fantasy. And like every really great mythical archetype, imaginative film-makers will continue from time to time to revitalize and reinterpret the text. In the meantime there are a legion of films to look back on, films that are intriguing not only in themselves, but in the peculiarly graphic way they relate to the development and the dispersal of sexual and social inhibitions. There can be few cinematic forms that chart the passage of permissiveness quite as strikingly as the vampire movie. It is a long and intricate path, full of false checks and equally deceptive advances, that winds its way through movie history, from the all-obscuring cloak that once shrouded the Count's nocturnal adventures in a delicate obscurity to the writhing bloody lesbian ecstasy of the Karnstein movies – and beyond.

THE VAMPIRE IN LEGEND AND LITERATURE

'A few questions on Transylvanian history'

A nineteenth-century engraving of a female vampire or succubus preying upon a sleeping man.

THE IDEA OF the vampire as we know it today is basically the fusion of two separate superstitions and fears, which from time to time still occur in their separate forms. The first essential characteristic of the vampire is that he or she is a person believed to be dead, who returns from the grave. The second is that he drinks human blood. Dividing the vampire's prime functions in this way perhaps makes it easier to understand the myth's universality.

After all, a whole gamut of human emotions — love, hate, guilt, incomprehension, fear — surround the response of the living towards the dead. And the equation of life with blood is as ancient as the oldest religion. In the vampire these two basic sources of human anxiety fuse into an image of the dead returning to steal the sacred life-fluid of the living.

But there is a further important dimension to the belief explored most cogently in Ernest Jones's *On the Nightmare*: Jones points out that blood is frequently an unconscious equivalent for semen and emphasizes the amount of sexual reference that abounds in even the oldest vampire lore. In Rumania the vampire was reputed to seduce young people of the opposite sex and indulge them sexually until they died of exhaustion. The Chaldeans believed that intercourse preceded the bloodsucking. The Indian Pisachas were said to ravish and feed off drunken or sleeping women. The Greek and Roman Lamias were both lovers and vampires: after their sexual conquest (and even after marriage) they would reveal themselves as flesh eaters. Indeed the wealth of material that is available makes it clear how difficult it is in many instances to distinguish between the sexual and violent function. There is only the thinnest of mythological lines between the vampire and the succubus, who was supposed to sap the sexual strength of mortals in their sleep. Frequently the two appear to be inseparable, with the demon performing both evil functions in close proximity. In fact, contrary to what might be expected, it was not until recent times that the sexual function of the vampire retreated further into the area of suggestion.

But it should be emphasized that there is an

Vlad the Impaler, a tyrannical fifteenth-century Wallachian prince, was reputed to have eaten meals in front of his impaled victims. Such barbarous acts have encouraged scholars to identify him with Stoker's Count Dracula, but his title of 'Dracul' and his Carpathian origins are the only real connections.

important distinction between the sexual paranoia at work here and the rampant pathological sexism that seems to have surrounded the idea of witches. In folklore the vampire has *never* been restricted to a single sex. Time after time it seems to appear simply in the guise most attractive to its victim. And whereas in so many reported outbreaks of witchcraft, the victim suffers some immediately painful loss or malady in no way ameliorated by sexual pleasure, the attentions of the vampire are frequently described with a lingering fascination and even delight: its visits are highly pleasurable, if contaminated. It is notable that whereas vampires are never accused of engendering impotence (quite the opposite), one of the most frequently recorded accusations of witchcraft was an interference with the male sexual function.

In psychological terms this distinction seems highly significant because it suggests that the pathology of vampire belief, although firmly rooted in a dualist soul/body split and fuelled by basic repression, is nowhere near as malig-

Bram Stoker, the business manager of Victorian actor Henry Irving; the circumstances underlying his creation of *Dracula* in 1897 are obscure, although it remains one of the most intensely imaginative works of popular fiction.

nant or destructive or male-orientated as the inner furies that drove people to hunt and destroy the women passing for witches.

In fact, compared to the witch-hunts of the late 15th and 16th centuries, vampire paranoia has been relatively minor and unimportant. The Roman Catholic Church seems to have treated it more as a minor sub-division of witchcraft, but this may have been partly because it had been stated that saints' bodies did not decompose, thus leading the Church into an awkward theological impasse on the vampire question. It was the Greek Orthodox Church which actively promoted the idea of vampires and taught that heretics risked this state after death. The best documented outbreak of vampirism in history took place in Meduegna in Yugoslavia in 1732. On this occasion a special delegation of dignitaries and high-ranking officers was actually sent into the stricken town and later signed a harrowing statement which described the disinterring of bodies gorged with new blood and numerous stakings. There is now no way of plausibly reconstructing the incident, but there cannot be much doubt that plague and drastic social deprivation could sometimes combine to bring about mass psychopathic episodes, a thousand times less congenial than the dreamy supernatural creatures of fiction.

The other authentic vampires are those mass murderers throughout history whose virtuosity has earned them a place in the vampire canon: Gilles de Rais, Elizabeth Bathory, Ed Gein, Peter Kurten and Fritz Haarmann were all at various periods responsible for extensive sadistic murders involving the consumption of human blood. Kurten and Haarmann, both Germans, came nearest in a strict biological sense to acting out the part of the vampire. Lang's film *M* was a stylish but bowdlerized account of Kurten's career, and Lommel's *Tenderness of the Wolves* featured a graphic portrayal of Haarmann.

The activities of the notorious Wisconsin necrophile Ed Gein were if anything more

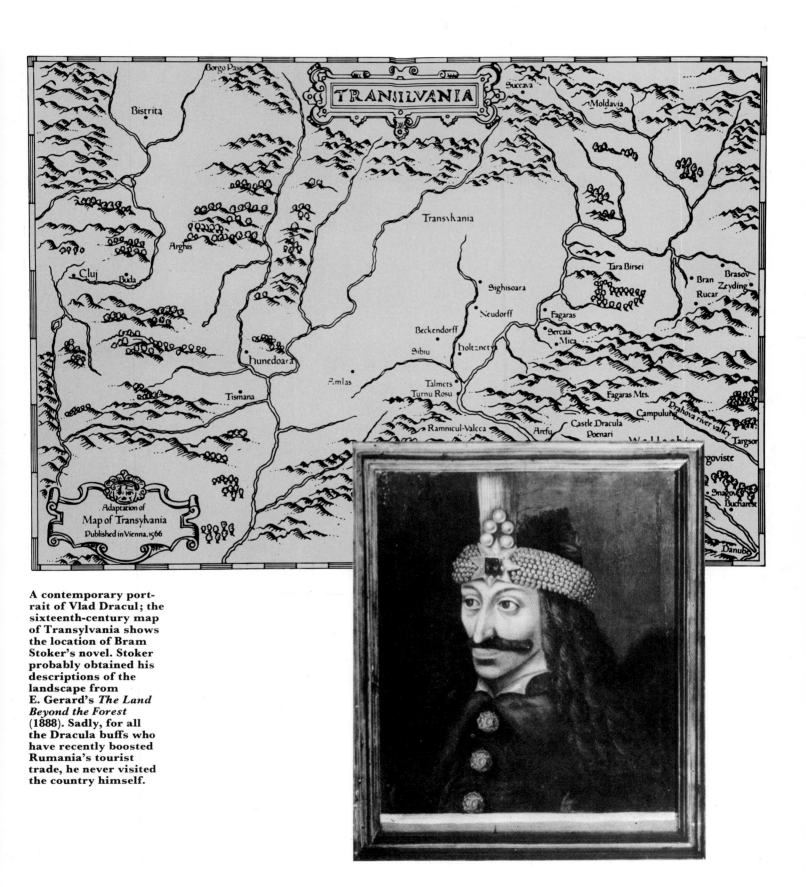

A contemporary portrait of Vlad Dracul; the sixteenth-century map of Transylvania shows the location of Bram Stoker's novel. Stoker probably obtained his descriptions of the landscape from E. Gerard's *The Land Beyond the Forest* (1888). Sadly, for all the Dracula buffs who have recently boosted Rumania's tourist trade, he never visited the country himself.

Roberts Blossom plays Ezra Cobb, a character closely modelled on the Wisconsin necrophile, Ed Gein, in *Deranged*. The real-life Gein was a pyschopath, whose practices came close to vampirism.

Some of Cobb's victims in *Deranged*.

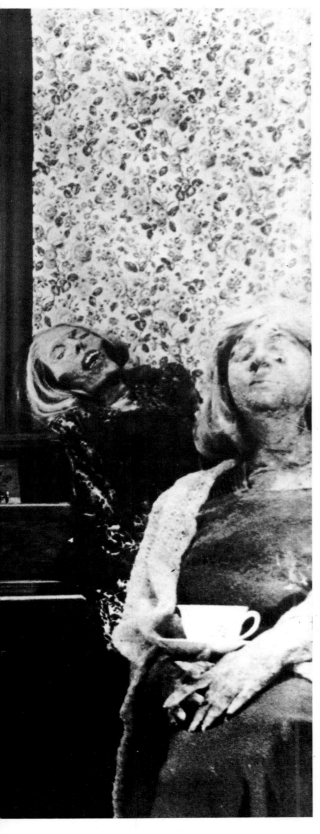

bizarre: he began by robbing graves and mummifying the bodies, then he started to wear human skin and pursue live victims. It was Gein who gave Robert Bloch the idea for *Psycho*, and his case has since been used by film-makers in *The Texas Chainsaw Massacre*, *Deranged* and several others. But, as should be clear from these examples, the true-life psychopath is very rarely a source for *vampire* movies. There is a world of difference between the psychological horror of mass murder and the dreamy romantic atmosphere of the undead. In fact, of the human vampires listed above, only Countess Bathory had any influence on the vampire cinema. Because of this it will be worth considering her story in a little detail, before leaving the annals of factual vampires altogether in favour of the real source of the vampire movie, which is literature.

Bathory has had a hold over the imagination of Gothic film-makers and writers that is greater than any other historical vampire figure. It is true that recent scholarship has established that Bram Stoker derived Dracula's name from a tyrannical fifteenth-century Wallachian Prince called Vlad Dracul. But Vlad's exploits have been ransacked since to reveal absolutely nothing that is truly vampiric (and a good deal that is completely irrelevant). With Bathory, on the other hand, the Dracula resonance is irresistible. Like the fictional Count, she was brought up 'in the horseshoe of the Carpathians' and Stoker probably learned of her existence during his British Museum researches from Sabine Baring-Gould's *The Book of Werewolves*.

She was born in 1560, the daughter of an ally of Ferdinand I of Hapsburg, and married Ferencz Nadasdy who, for most of their marriage, left her in the privacy she preferred in numerous isolated castles. There, over a period of years, protected from any interference by her powerful connections, Elizabeth Bathory pursued an obsession that seems to be unequalled in history. As soon as she arrived somewhere, even for a short visit, her first

Bathory became a standard vampire villainess in Paul Naschy's *Walpurgis* series; here, an original poster for *El Retorno de Walpurgis*.

A contemporary portrait of Countess Elizabeth Bathory, the 'Bloody Countess'.

Opposite: **Ingrid Pitt in Hammer's distorted account of Countess Bathory's sadistic career. In this film version,** *Countess Dracula,* **the sole motive for her bloody deeds is eternal youth.**

concern was to establish a suitable torture chamber where the victims' cries would not attract attention. Usually it would be a cellar or a high-turreted room, on one occasion it was the laundry. Her domestic staff was organized with the express purpose of finding a suitable pool of young female victims, and sometimes she moved from one castle to another simply because the supply of young girls from the surrounding peasantry was exhausted.

Bathory was not simply a murderess, she was a murder factory. As many as six hundred girls over a period of hardly more than fifteen years may have been fed into her voracious recreation chamber. She had a range of apparatus that included all the traditional horrors, but seemed to prefer the most direct means at her disposal. Sometimes she would participate directly; at other times she howled instructions from her carefully positioned high chair. The reliable accounts of her trial and the correspondence relating to the case (including some of Bathory's own letters and writing) are so harrowing that they were suppressed until the 18th century. Even today, Valentine Penrose's biography *The Bloody Countess* makes chilling reading.

The Countess is reminiscent of the Dracula archetype in many ways. In the first place, she does literally seem to have been responsible for the spoliation of the families around her castle even though she was only concerned with young girls. These hapless communities had no defence whatsoever against their powerful overlord, they were simply informed of 'disappearances'. Like a true vampire, Bathory was frequently driven on by her blood frenzy to richer pastures. And she also seems to have believed that the blood of her victims could keep her skin pale and her body healthy. In the circumstances this was little more than a rationalization of her own psychopathic bouts (after which we are told she would orgasm almost into unconsciousness), but it adds an uncanny dimension to the appalling facts. Finally she was bricked up in her castle while still alive after a court sentenced her to life imprisonment.

All these things, together with the all-pervading air of sexuality, have naturally excited the attention of film-makers: there are at least four official appearances by Bathory in the vampire cinema (*Countess Dracula*, *Daughters of Darkness*, *La Noche de Walpurgis* and its sequel *El Returno de Walpurgis*), plus a legion of films that draw heavily on the story.

Apart from the Countess the prototype of the demonic aristocrat screen vampire, prior to Bram Stoker's crystallization of the theme in *Dracula*, was Lord Byron. Byron deliberately cultivated the Gothic image of the satanic rake and his notoriety was such that news of him – both real and imagined – spread rapidly throughout Europe during and after his lifetime. The vampire had a particular fascination for Byron, indeed he seemed to favour it as a description of himself: he was described by Blessington as often in conversation 'taking up the part of a fallen or exiled being . . . existing under a curse, pre-doomed to a fate . . . that he seemed determined to fulfil.'

Even so, it is possible that Byron would not have been so influential in this respect if it had

Delphine Seyrig in Harry Kumel's remarkable recreation of the Bathory myth, *Daughters of Darkness.*

Opposite: **Some of the sadistic, lesbian mood of the Bathory legend is conveyed in Jean Rollin's** *Requiem pour un Vampire.*

not been for his famous encounter with Shelley at the Villa Diodati in the summer of 1816.

This was the epoch-making occasion that gave rise to Mary Shelley's *Frankenstein* and the crucial Dracula-source *The Vampyre*, conceived by Byron himself, and written by John Polidori. But until very recently accounts of what happened at Diodati have been sabotaged by the drastic nineteenth-century bowdlerization that dogs every attempt to chronicle the life of Shelley. The usual impression conveyed is of a jolly summer party at which the guests held a kind of ghost-story competition because it was wet. Even the dreadful prologue of Whale's film *The Bride of Frankenstein* continues to perpetuate the myth that Diodati was a charming gathering of turn-of-the-century elegance where Mary would startle and amuse her guests with the latest product of her adolescent imagination.

In fact Diodati was an emotional whirlpool of such complexity that even Shelley's most

In 1819 Byron wrote rather disingenuously to the editor of Gaglianani's *Journal* in Paris, disclaiming his part in the composition of *The Vampyre*; much mystery still surrounds its conception during the Diodati summer of 1816.

Sir, In various numbers of your Journal I have seen mentioned a work entitled "the Vampire" with the addition of my name as that of the Author. — I am not the author, and never heard of the work in question until now. In a more recent paper I perceive a formal annunciation of "the Vampire" with the addition of an account of my "residence in the Island of Mitylene" an Island which I have occasionally sailed by in the course of travelling some years ago through the Levant — and where I should have no objection to reside — but where I have never yet resided. — — Neither of these per= =formances are mine — and I presume that it is neither unjust nor ungracious to request that you will favour me by contradicting the adver= =tisement to which I allude. — If the book is

The other literary
result of the Diodati
summer: Mary
Shelley's *Frankenstein*;
frontispiece of the 1831
edition.

brilliant biographer, the aptly named Richard Holmes, has not completely unravelled it. What is certain is this: Shelley was in a state of economic and psychological desperation, having eloped from England with two women, the half-sisters Mary Wollstonecraft and Claire Clairmont; that, in some way yet to be completely clarified, he was intensely involved with each of them and they with him. Moreover Claire had also embarked on a turbulent sexual affair with Byron, and considerable animosity was developing between her and Mary; Byron himself was accompanied by a violently possessive male companion, the physician John Polidori. It would be hard to construct a more potentially explosive gathering, especially when you consider the immediate attraction between Byron and Shelley who were meeting for the first time.

Shelley had been a devotee of horrific literature since his youth, and terrorized his sisters with tales of vampires. The setting of Diodati is spectacularly eerie even today, with clumps of trees and grass sloping away to the icy ethereal stillness of Lake Geneva spread out below it. Only a few miles away by boat lies the astonishing medieval castle of Chillon with some of the most forbidding dungeons in the world, where Byron sardonically carved his name. The pages of the Shelley diary are suggestively missing for this entire period. But we know that on one occasion Shelley ran shrieking from the room because he had seen living eyes on Mary's breasts. In the circumstances it does not seem so surprising that Diodati brought to fruition both the central Gothic literary myths that were later utilized by the cinema.

The genesis of *Frankenstein* is fully (though unreliably) documented by Mary herself. Of *The Vampyre* we know less except that Byron appears to have concocted it as a kind of narcissistic amusement. Much later, Polidori – in a vain attempt to gain advantage from his abortive association with the poet – fleshed out the plot and sent it to the *New Monthly Maga-*

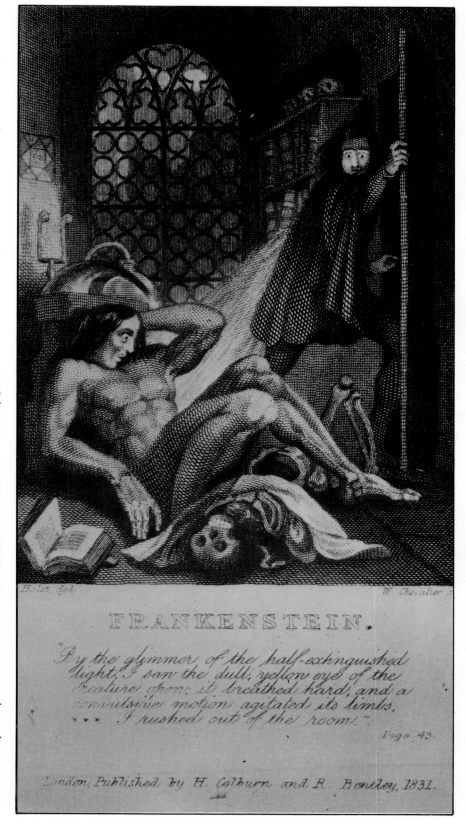

FRANKENSTEIN.

"*By the glimmer of the half-extinguished light, I saw the dull, yellow eye of the creature open; it breathed hard, and a convulsive motion agitated its limbs.* *... I rushed out of the room.*"

Page 43.

London, Published by H. Colburn and R. Bentley, 1831.

zine. It was published under Byron's name in 1819 and gained a sensational vogue throughout Europe.

The Vampyre is not easy to read today, but its conception of the aristocratic male decadent who preys on the blood of young girls marked the first triumphant appearance of the vampire in Gothic fiction. For the first time the vampire had ceased to be a ravening fiend, and becomes instead a seductive, charismatic anti-hero, introduced at the height of the London season, touring the continent and finally slaughtering his companion's sister. The appearance of 'Lord Ruthwen' is highly suggestive. He has piercing eyes, a gaunt, unusual appearance and a strange underlying melancholy. There is

nothing new about this, it is the stock description of the 'fatal man' which Byron had lifted from the pages of the popular novels and turned into a major character cult. But Polidori achieved the unmistakable coup of converting this character into a vampire, and this was all that was needed for Count Dracula to be born.

The direct sources of Stoker's book, published in 1897, have been the cause of much speculation, because the author left little evidence. However, he could hardly have been unaware of Polidori's work which had been transformed into a successful play throughout Europe and America, and initiated dozens of imitations. There is also the interesting fact that Polidori was an uncle of Dante Gabriel

Rossetti, a neighbour of Stoker's in Cheyne Walk. A few attempts have been made to find some psychological explanation for *Dracula* in Stoker's past. The possibility that his employer, the actor Henry Irving, influenced the characterization of the Count has been postulated unconvincingly.

More recently a paper appeared in the *British Journal of Medical Psychology* by an American, Seymour Shuster, on 'Dracula and Surgically Induced Trauma in Children'. It proposed that *Dracula* resulted 'from the long-repressed anxiety relating to the author's childhood experiences with doctors' and proceeded to draw some parallels between a child's nightmarish impression of hospitals and the opening section of the novel: the journey to an unfamiliar place, the fear of going to sleep in strange rooms, the jabbing with a sharp instrument, the fact that Harker is carried back to his room unconscious by Dracula (i.e. wheeled back from the operating table). Unfortunately Shuster is relying entirely on supposition and at times his suggestions become incredibly strained. He is not even able to state for sure if Stoker ever visited a hospital as a child. It seems that, until real biographical evidence turns up, there is no great value to be derived from this kind of speculation, although the motives behind it are understandable.

Because Dracula has proved to be one of the most unstoppable literary conceptions of all

Bran Castle, which still stands in the Carpathians, has many of the features of Stoker's Castle Dracula.

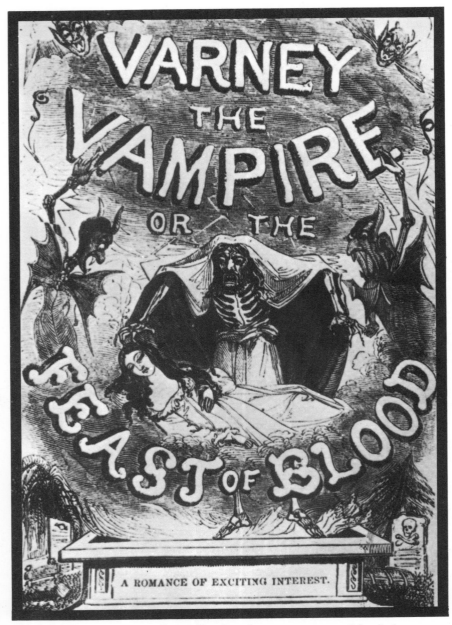

A ROMANCE OF EXCITING INTEREST.

of immense unconscious power, weaving a spell of sex, blood and death around the reader, which remains quite unaffected by time. On one level at least, the character of the Count can be construed as the great submerged force of Victorian libido breaking out to punish the repressive society which had imprisoned it; one of the more appalling things that the Count perpetually does to the matronly women of his Victorian enemies (in the novel and in the best of the films) is to make them sensual.

But with brilliant ingenuity, Stoker disguises his anti-father and anti-Christ in smooth anglophile charm. In one of the very few biographical facts we have, Harry Ludlam quotes Stoker as often laughing to his friends about 'how he made his vampire monster wait hand and foot on Jonathan Harker . . . at the castle.' Even when Dracula is about to pitch Harker out of the front door into a pack of wolves he speaks 'with a sweet courtesy which made me rub my eyes it seemed so real.'

Dracula is presented to the reader in the form of a dossier, a technique borrowed by Stoker from Wilkie Collins, which adds something to its pseudo-scientific air of authenticity. Harker's journals, which constitute the novel's ingenious opening section, centre upon the chronicler's gradually dawning realization that he is confronted with a man – Count Dracula – and a world – Dracula's domain in Transylvania – that his prim Victorian common sense is at a loss to comprehend.

Harker is a solicitor's agent on a business mission in a far-flung corner of the world to service a mysterious and wealthy client. From the beginning, the lawyer's somewhat mundane fears and preoccupations contrast pitifully with the bizarre nexus of other-worldly ideas and associations surrounding him. Yet when Dracula chooses to meet Harker on his own legalistic ground, even here the Count proves to be superior. Harker has to admit his opponent 'would have made a wonderful solicitor', and is completely outwitted when he tries to smuggle some letters out of the castle. Right up to the

time. By far the most successful of the great Gothic villains, including Frankenstein, the Count has for nearly a hundred years rampaged his way through publishing, the theatre, the cinema, comic books, television, popular music and merchandizing of every kind from bubble gum and cereal to iced lollies. He is one of a tiny number of completely universal and international fictional characters. Like Sherlock Holmes, who was created around the same time and endowed with something of the same mysterious literary energy, he has spawned a whole undergrowth of literary imitations, modernizations and bastardizations.

Dracula's success as a character is no historical accident. The novel in which he appears is one of the most extraordinary works of popular fiction ever written, an astonishing culmination of the sado-erotic strains and stresses of the entire Victorian age. It is a book

Thomas Preskett Press adapted Byron's/Polidori's conception to mount a successful 800-page serial in 1847; *Varney the Vampire*, a 'penny dreadful', related the lurid adventures of Sir Francis Varney.

last, Dracula is somehow able to preserve the elaborate charade of host-and-guest, even when his victim knows he is about to be killed. This duel of wits is crucial to the novel because, having established its villain's demonic cunning, it is structurally necessary to reduce him to a sinister background presence in the plot that now unfolds.

Leaving Harker clambering perilously down the precipitous wall of Castle Dracula, the action of *Dracula* shifts to the apparently trivial concerns of Harker's fiancée, Mina, and her friend, Lucy, back in England. In chilling contrast to the opening section, the pages of the novel are now filled with the trite concerns of two marriage-obsessed Victorian girls. We read of proposals and hobbies and of how 'it must be so nice to see strange countries.' But it soon becomes clear that all is not well behind the stifling veneer: the first vindication derives

from one of Lucy's rejected suitors, who maintains a lunatic asylum. His patient Renfield has begun to behave oddly, eating spiders and birds and flies. There is nothing to connect this with the Count, but it is an echo.

This is all part of the genius of *Dracula*'s conception. After the strange surreal terror of Castle Dracula, Stoker deliberately submerges us in a sumptuous Victorian comedy of manners and romance. The fact that our information is gained from letters and diaries augments this effect, because we are forced to pursue the indiscriminate trivia of dinner parties and afternoon walks and trousseaux. But suddenly, like a sumptuous colour film shredding and emulsifying in the projector gate, the images before us start to jar and shudder, the colours bleach and the whole smooth façade begins to dissolve. Lucy, the most hearty and frivolous of the two girls, becomes morbid and obsessive;

Overleaf: **Hammer juxtaposed Ingrid Pitt in this credit sequence from *Countess Dracula* with a more authentic representation of the deeds of the 'Bloody Countess'.**

the weather changes to a gloomy turbulence ('Everything is grey,' Mina writes, 'grey rock . . . grey clouds . . . grey sea . . . the horizon is lost in a grey mist'); a mysterious ship lands in Whitby with a dead man lashed to the mast. Lucy is locked in her room at night but scrambles to get out, she grows weak and hysterical, betraying all the skeletal symptoms that today we would associate with anorexia. Finally, as she is dying and begging her fiancé Arthur for a final kiss, Van Helsing, the ambiguous doctor who has been called in to preside over the case's more unusual aspects, catches Arthur by the neck and hurls him across the room with both hands.

This grotesque parody of a Dickensian death scene is only the beginning. After Lucy's death her sexually tormented fiancé is forced by Van Helsing to track his love to her unquiet grave, where 'she seemed like a nightmare of Lucy . . . the pointed teeth, the bloodstained voluptuous mouth . . . the whole carnal and unspiritual appearance.' Arthur is compelled to drive in the stake 'deeper and deeper . . . whilst the blood from the pierced heart welled and spurted up around it.' It is the climax of what has become a monstrous inversion of the whole Victorian courtship. Like any other novelist of his day Stoker was unable to describe the *real* climax of a courtship. He could not write about a sexual relationship between a man and a woman, but all the tormented anguish that surrounded this forbidden subject erupts into the distorted tension and violence that ultimately links Arthur and his vampire lover.

It soon becomes clear that Count Dracula is playing with his opponents, rather as if they were a herd of cows for his consumption. Mina becomes his second blood-bank. As with Lucy, the men desperately transfuse their blood into her during the day and Dracula samples it at night. He even compels Mina to drink from his own chest, thus ensuring her contamination unless he can be destroyed. The turnabout in the balance of power in *Dracula* comes late and takes agonizingly long to accomplish. But finally the infection that has begun to sweep through England in the person of the Count is forced back to the outlying realms of Transylvania where it is eventually destroyed. If the Victorians shivered, it may have been because they rightly wondered how long the sexual energy that Dracula represented could be kept safely out of sight across the sea and 'beyond the forest'.

As Dracula's opponent, Stoker had created the impassioned eccentric Dutch theologist Van Helsing, an occultist and a detective who utilizes a whole paraphernalia of esoteric devices to trap his foe. Like Sherlock Holmes, one may suspect that Van Helsing derives a good deal of his power from the fact that he is able to represent religion and science at a time – the begin-

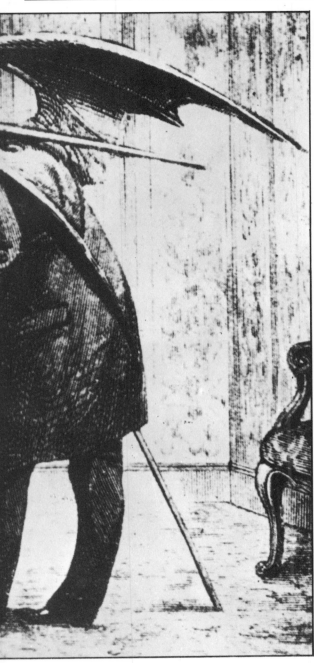

A nineteenth-century
engraving in which a
woman fervently
embraces a winged
male vampire, with
cane and bowler. It was
Bram Stoker who first
popularized the con-
nection between the
human vampire and
the vampire bat.

appears anonymously one hundred and fifty years after her funeral to insinuate herself into a lonely Styrian family who shelter her at the request of a mysterious noblewoman. Although shorter than *Dracula* and finally less substantial, *Carmilla* is deftly constructed and superbly atmospheric. Its vampire is a beautiful child-like girl, who moves and acts with a dream-like languidness and somehow remains extremely ambiguous throughout: she is prone to fainting fits and desperate little bursts of lesbian emotion that make her frighteningly sympathetic. At one point the young female narrator describes how Carmilla would take her hand and 'hold it with a fond pressure, renewed again and again; blushing softly, gazing in my face with languid and burning eyes, and breathing so fast that her dress rose and fell with the tumultuous respiration. It was like the ardour of a lover . . . and she would whisper almost in sobs "You are mine, you shall be mine . . ."'

This cloying, almost sickly, atmosphere of furtive girlish passion was conveyed by Le Fanu with considerable economy, and much later it was taken up by the makers of vampire movies with understandable relish. Next to *Dracula* itself, *Carmilla* has been adapted for the screen more often than any other work of vampire fiction, and Stoker himself, who had read *Carmilla*, used something of Le Fanu's insidiously sensual style. When Harker encounters the giggling vampire women in Dracula's castle: 'I longed with a wicked burning desire that they would kiss me with those red lips . . . There was a deliberate voluptuousness which was both thrilling and repulsive and as she arched her neck she actually licked her lips like an animal . . .'.

As this passage reveals, the difference between Bram Stoker and so many other writers of vampire fiction, including the prolific Thomas Preskett Prest, was that his background in the theatre had made him, not just an exponent, but a master of dramatic effect. It is not surprising that once he hit on a theme as visually arresting and sexually liberating as the demon aristocrat vampire, what he eventually wrote should have proved irresistible to the film-makers of the 20th century.

ning of the 20th century – when the two systems were about to split indissolubly apart. In Van Helsing the Christian vampire hunter, and in Holmes the moralistic, sometimes mystical, detective, the two are fleetingly reunited.

With Dracula installed firmly in the popular imagination, it was only a matter of time before the *femme fatale*, or 'fatal woman', the other stock literary device of Gothic fiction, would assume vampire characteristics. And in fact this had already happened in Le Fanu's *Carmilla* (1872), which represents, with Stoker's novel, the other central source of cinematic vampires. Carmilla was also an aristocrat, the Countess Mircalla, who re-

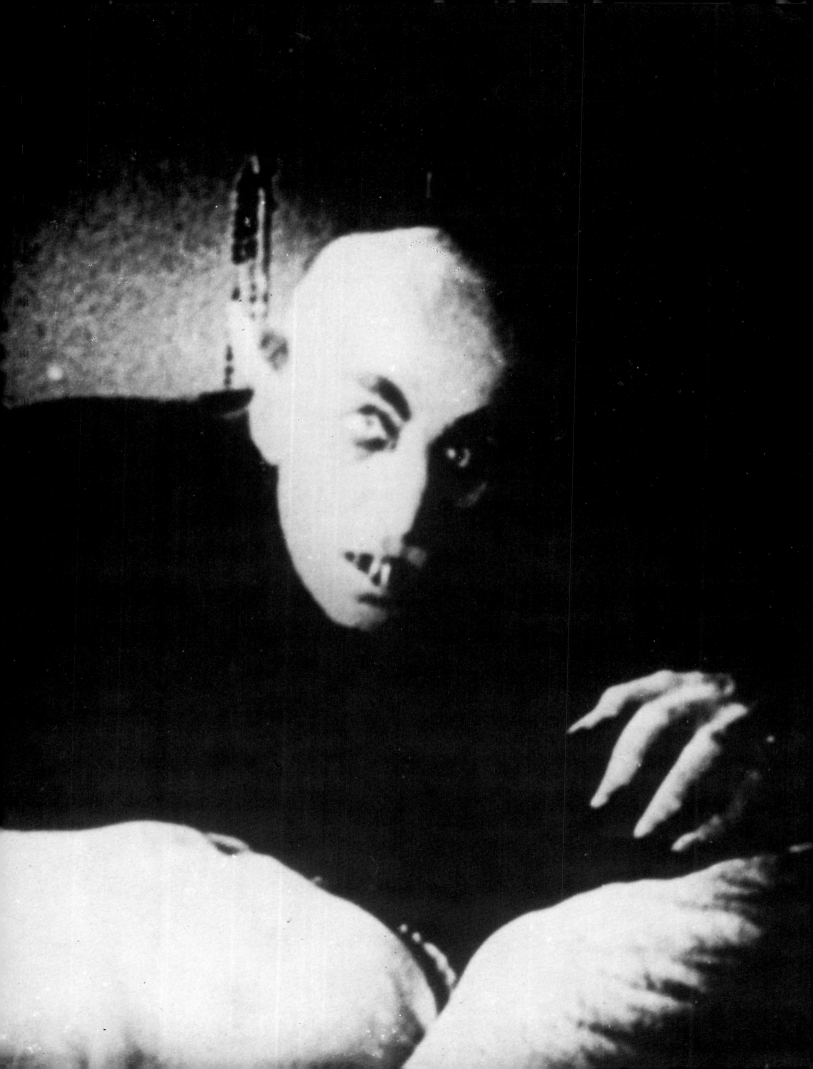

ORIGINS OF THE VAMPIRE MOVIE

'My master the Count'

The mysterious actor
Max Schreck as Count
Orlock in F. W.
Murnau's pirated
version of Stoker's
novel: *Nosferatu.*

THERE ARE SEVERAL tricky problems inherent in discussing the earliest substantial manifestations of a much-loved screen genre. The first products of the cinema were treated with scant care, prints of many films up to the era of sound and beyond are often in bad condition and frequently lost altogether. But the worst problem does not arise from rarity value. Any film enthusiast must learn to live with that. It lies rather in the tendency of film historians to over-value the distant past at the expense of the recent past, the present and even the future.

The over-protectiveness is quite forgivable. After all, any writer will want to overcome the blind assertions of movie advertising. Moreover, the cinema is so intimately connected with our own personal history, is so much a promulgator of nostalgia and half-remembered emotion, that it is peculiarly susceptible to time-distortion, prejudicing us in favour of the earliest movies we have seen. Every attempt to discriminate between movies reflects a certain subjective bias.

Yet the recent history of film criticism has, I think, proved how dangerous subjective bias can be if it is given too free a reign, or considered too important a factor in the overall consideration of film. No field has suffered more in this respect than the horror movie. Contemporary horror movies have been shunned and reviled so frequently by the critics of their own time, especially in England, that such notices had almost become a ritual act until relatively recently.

Consequently, the horror devotee will not find it difficult to sympathize with those French and English critics who advocate a suspension of all value judgments in favour of a proper and sober examination of the films themselves. The vampire movie is in fact admirably suited to this procedure, and if I use subjective judgments in discussing the films, they are not intended to denote some abstract and lordly perspective, but simply as an indication of how far I think an individual film will reward proper scrutiny. It seems fair to add my own preconception that a narrative film is worth consideration exactly to the extent that it is 'entertaining', and I use the word to indicate *any* quality, whether intellectual (thematic, semantic, syntactic, etc.) or emotional (amusing, exciting, sympathetic, etc.) in which I can find relevance.

On this basis, it seems to me that, with some notable exceptions, the earliest vampire movies have been slightly overvalued: their rarity, their antiquity and in some cases their naivety have endowed them with an aura that is often undeserved and occasionally ludicrous. Few would deny that the vampire benefited from the introduction of sound, and I suspect that even the staunchest devotees of monochrome might find it difficult to argue the superiority of the black-and-white vampire movie on a film-for-film basis. The tradition of the vampire movie, as of vampire literature, has only marginally been one of suggestion. The vampire is a grossly physical being, a palpable, fleshy entity, not a shadow.

A number of obscure early American, German and British shorts have wrongly found their way into filmographies of the vampire. Surprising as it may seem, neither *Vampires of the Coast* (1909), *The Vampire* (1911), *The Vampire's Tower* (Italian, 1913), *The Vampire's Clutch* (1914), *Vampires of the Night* (1914), *Tracked by a Vampire* (1914), nor *A Village Vampire* (1916) have any supernatural content at all. Many of these movies used the word vampire simply as an innocuous alternative for *femme fatale* or vamp. There is, however, one British short, *The Vampire* (1913), in which a vampire woman in India kills two men, but the metamorphosis is into a snake rather than a bat.

The first important vampire movie was made in Germany in 1922 by F. W. Murnau; appropriately enough, *Nosferatu* was a pirated version of Stoker's *Dracula*. Indeed the production has all the marks of a potboiler, mounted so casually and quickly that nobody appears to have realized how vulnerable it was to legal action. It was released in March 1922 by the Prana Company of Berlin, and news of the film reached Bram Stoker's widow Florence only two months later. Although a feeble attempt has been made to disguise the source

Count Orlock (Max Schreck) in his Carpathian castle prior to his journey to Bremen in a ship laden with coffins.

by changing a few names and altering the setting, she was easily able to bring an action for the infringement of copyright. The company made a succession of appeals that were uniformly denied, and then proceeded to go bankrupt. The court's final decision came in July 1925, when all prints were ordered to be destroyed. Most of them subsequently disappeared, but fortunately the makers had managed to sell the negative abroad. Florence was able to prevent it opening in London in 1925, but it surfaced again three years later, and finally reached American screens twelve months after that.

Heretical as it may seem, it is hard not to feel a sneaking sympathy for Florence Stoker's objections to the film. She was not unsympathetic to the idea of an adaptation of *Dracula*; indeed, only three years after the making of *Nosferatu* she sanctioned Hamilton Deane's play, and she was still alive to see Lugosi's incarnation of the Count in 1931. But Murnau's film had been undertaken with scant respect for the original or its author.

The scriptwriter Henrik Galeen sets his action in Bremen in 1838, where a young estate agent, Hutter, is commissioned to visit Count Orlock (the same pseudonym that Bogdanovich would bestow on Boris Karloff half a century later for the disturbing horror pastiche *Targets*). Hutter encounters peasants' warnings and is terrorized by Orlock, who then leaves his castle in the Carpathians and sets sail for Bremen in a ship laden with coffins. The ship arrives in Bremen harbour ominously empty and it is not long before a plague of rats threatens the city. Meanwhile, Hutter's wife is troubled by her husband's disappearance while his employer goes insane and is placed in an asylum. When Hutter breaks out of the castle to warn his wife, she conceives the scheme of seducing the vampire until he disintegrates in the light of morning. The plan works but Hutter is left with only her corpse, after the vampire has disintegrated in the sunlight.

Almost everyone who has seen *Nosferatu*,

Hutter explores Orlock's castle in *Nosferatu.*

whatever his or her opinion of the film, seems to agree that its strongest feature is the vampire himself. Nothing could be further from the image of the Count as Stoker wrote it and subsequent film-makers interpreted it. The well-groomed, demonic vampire of Stoker is transformed into a skeletal, contorted monster, who shuffles with senile purpose in and out of frame. He resembles an animated corpse far more tellingly than the whole parade of Hollywood zombies who were to succeed him: the long fingers tapering away into little sticks of bone and nail; the broad, domed, hairless scalp with grotesquely stretched pale skin; the mongoloid pointed ears, staring eyes and gap-toothed mouth. There is something highly suggestive about Orlock's movements in the film, especially when he avoids the theatrical gesture and keeps his extraordinary hands pinned close to his side, alongside the black, tightly-fitting tunic. In these moments his walk seems quite inorganic, as though the little animation he has is simply some wild reflex of those pouched glaring eyes.

Considering the wealth of ideas and associations in Murnau's other work, it might have been expected that he would build happily on all the sado-erotic connotations of the vampire, but in fact his film studiously ignores these aspects. Even the visually arresting climax in which the vampire is destroyed by sunlight, and Hutter throws himself upon his all-sacrificing wife, is handled in a theatrical and symbolic fashion that somehow evokes Wagner rather than Gothic fiction.

It is a pity that Murnau's own attitude to the project, and the reasons why he undertook it, remain thoroughly obscure. The late Edgar Ulmer, his close friend and assistant, was pressed on this question by the French cinema publication *Midi-Minuit Fantastique*. He replied that Murnau was never a great enthusiast of the fantasy cinema, and a dominant influence behind *Nosferatu* was the Swedish director Mauritz Stiller whose work gave Murnau the idea of using negative film during Hutter's

In spite of its subject matter and its director, Murnau's *Nosferatu* (inset) only occasionally utilized the expressionist imagery which had been such a notable feature of Robert Wiene's classic early horror film *The Cabinet of Dr Caligari*. Cesar, the black-clad somnambulist of Wiene's film bears more resemblance than Orlock to succeeding generations of screen Draculas.

A Belgian poster for the original Hammer *Dracula*, directed by Terence Fisher.

ride in the vampire carriage. Ulmer also suggested intriguingly that the well-known actor Max Schreck may not have played the vampire at all, at least in the film's most famous sequences. Ulmer maintained that Murnau persuaded his close friend the scriptwriter Hans Ramo to act in the film. More mysteries seem to surround the shooting of *Nosferatu* than ever appear on the screen.

Even in its expressionist qualities, *Nosferatu* exhibits none of the shadow play of the earlier *Caligari*. The few studio interiors are inexplicably plain and sterile. Only Orlock, advancing awesomely behind his huge black shadow (and therefore incidentally breaking every rule of vampire lore) gives the interiors a proper expressionist emphasis.

But in one vital respect *Nosferatu* did point prophetically and courageously to the true destiny of the vampire picture. This was in its use of exteriors. If there is one magic ingredient of the vampire genre in literature or the cinema, one that sometimes even supersedes the vampire himself, it is the *landscape* he inhabits. Stoker knew this perfectly well and poured all his energies into a portrayal of the Transylvanian terrain in the first few chapters of *Dracula*. It did not matter in the slightest that Stoker had never been to Transylvania (though the more ardent researchers into Vlad and the country's history frequently seem to forget this fact). He was a great Gothic writer, and he knew how to evoke a *feeling* from landscape which is the key tool of anyone working in the field.

In the cinema the same tool was to become central to the whole conception of cinematic Gothic. The vampire may be the active agent of terror, but the passive agent is the landscape he inhabits. It does not matter whether this is a wooded English hillside, a lonely stretch of east European moorland or the windswept Baroque of off-season Ostend. In certain circumstances it might even be a contemporary urban setting, though the failure of Hammer's last two Dracula films (*Dracula A.D. 1972* and

The Satanic Rites of Dracula) indicates the magnitude of the difficulties involved. The important point is that the landscape must be utilized to supply a quality of remoteness without which the vampire might become completely mundane. The undead may shun sunlight, but they remain, in narrative form, a Gothic creation, and consequently their relation with Gothic landscape is an intimate one. The cinema would have to wait many years before the creature was restored to its natural element.

Surprisingly, after *Nosferatu*, the vampire moved right to the back of the movie stage. This is not easy to explain, considering there were around five versions of *Dr. Jekyll and Mr. Hyde* made in Hollywood before 1930 alone. Stevenson's premise may have been regarded by producers as more scientific. The possibility also exists that the morality of the vampire clashed with the prevailing moral stance of the American movie industry at this time. Human villains were acceptable, as were monsters, but where the two combined, as in so many pictures of Lon Chaney, there was always a streak of tragedy and pathos. The vampire may in theory be a tragic figure, but it is

Lon Chaney (here with Jacqueline Logan) plays the hunchbacked ape-man assistant to a mad doctor in *A Blind Bargain*. Chaney planned to extend his talent for the grotesque to portrayals of both Dracula and Frankenstein.

Lon Chaney, with Edna Tichenor as his daughter, plays the pretend vampire in Tod Browning's *London After Midnight*.

pitiless and it disdains pity; the audience is rarely asked to share its suffering. It is a very long way from Quasimodo and the Phantom of the Opera to Count Dracula.

Lon Chaney however intended to make the transition. The son of deaf mute parents, his skill at mime and macabre physical contortion made his collaboration with film-maker Tod Browning throughout the 1920s highly suitable. Browning's history was equally romantic: he had run away from school to join a circus and, in the late 1890s, travelled throughout the world with various acts. After a brief spell as an actor, he was soon making features, and came across Chaney eking out a living on the Hollywood sidelines. A few years later in 1925, when Chaney had become a big star, he began a fruitful partnership with Browning at MGM.

Browning and Chaney both shared a sense of the macabre, though their taste never properly extended into the area of Gothic. In 1927 the pair combined to make *London After Midnight*, a quasi-vampire picture which is one of the most frustrating of all lost films. The stills show Chaney at his most energetically demonic, with wires that make his eyes bulge like poached eggs, pointed chin and wisps of long fair hair hanging down from a tall black hat. It is an image that has somehow survived in the popular imagination, even after the movie from which it is taken has been destroyed. It has the same striking power as the similarly tailored *Caligari*. But the evidence is that, to all intents and purposes, *London After Midnight* was not really a vampire film at all. In Browning's script, which he remade in 1935, the vampire is actually an impersonation to trap a gang of criminals, and all the supernatural events are explained away at the end in the worst tradition of Mrs. Radcliffe. The silent audience was not thought to be prepared to accept what Browning called the 'horrible impossible', though it is difficult to see why Mr. Hyde did not fit into the category.

If the pattern of Chaney's subsequent career had been different, then it is possible the whole history of horror films would have to be rewritten. Because by 1927 to the American public Chaney was 'horror', even though the

word in its film sense was yet to be invented. He had been the hunchbacked ape-man assistant of a mad doctor in *A Blind Bargain* (1922), the mad waxworks curator in *While Paris Sleeps* (1923), Quasimodo in *The Hunchback of Notre Dame* (1923), a psychopathic surgeon in *The Monster* (1925), the demented phantom in *The Phantom of the Opera* (1925) and countless others.

Together, Browning and Chaney had pioneered a new kind of genre, even though judging by Browning's scruples over *London After Midnight*, they were as uncertain as anyone else about what form it would take. With the development of sound, Browning was in a prime position to develop his taste for the macabre and it was his intention that Chaney should assist him. By this time the director was installed at Universal, and Chaney had made the successful break into sound pictures. *The Unholy Three*, his sound debut was, according

Conrad Nagel points to the tell-tale sign of the undead in one of the most famous of all lost films, *London After Midnight*.

One of the very few
modern horror films
to betray the influence
of Dreyer's *Vampyr* is
Sidney Hayers' *Night
of the Eagle*, adapted
by scriptwriter
Richard Matheson
from Fritz Leiber's
classic story of the
supernatural *Conjure
Wife*. Janet Blair plays
a suburban housewife
drawn into the practice
of witchcraft.

was at his best conveying physical contortion
and deformity, attributes that were ideally
suited to the emotional emphasis of silent
movies, but could never play so crucial a role
in the sound era. And they are attributes which
are supremely wrong in the vampire.

Meanwhile, as the Universal era was
getting underway, a co-production team involving extraordinary talents had embarked
on a fully-fledged vampire project in France.
Dreyer's *Vampyr*, which was shot on and off over
a period of one year from the early spring of
1930 to the summer of 1931, is a sensational
parenthesis in the history of the horror movie.
Both in theme and style it achieved an unprecedented sophistication. Indeed thirty-five
years had to elapse before its most daring
technical effect – the burial of the camera –
would be successfully copied by another director (Roger Corman in *The Premature Burial*).

The circumstances of *Vampyr's* production
were in themselves exceptional. At the height
of his success with *The Passion of Joan of Arc*, the
Danish film-maker Carl Dreyer was at a high
society ball in Paris where he was introduced to
an admirer, Baron Nicolas de Gunzburg.
Dreyer decided he wanted to mount a film
around the Baron, a youthful patron of the
arts and together they set about combing
supernatural fiction for a suitable subject. At
about the same time as Universal were beginning preparations for *Dracula*, they came
across Le Fanu's collection of short stories
In a Glass Darkly, and predictably the story
Carmilla attracted Dreyer's attention.

In the end almost all that Dreyer took from
Le Fanu was the idea of a female vampire and
a hero who collects supernatural experiences.
The latter was to be the Baron's part, and he
also agreed to produce the film. Billed under
the pseudonym Julian West to avoid family
embarrassment, he played David Gray, a
sensitive young man who wanders in search of
strange phenomena. Sybille Schmitz was sum-
moned from Berlin to play the threatened
heroine, and Maurice Schutz took the part of

to one critic, the most successful transition to
the new medium since Greta Garbo. Preparations were afoot at Universal to star the new
Chaney in a completely original American
movie concept adapted from a successful play.
He was to play Count Dracula.

Exactly at this point in his career, Chaney
was robbed of the chance of breaking out of his
habitual range of characters. Before and after
shooting *The Unholy Three* he had been
confined to bed with what he and his public
thought was pneumonia. His occasionally
husky voice was explained as the result of
irritation caused by artificial snow particles on
an earlier movie, *Thunder*. In fact it was cancer
of the throat. Chaney died on 25 August 1930,
only two months after the release of his first
sound role and a matter of five weeks before
Tod Browning began shooting the opening
segments of *Dracula*.

There can be very little doubt that, if Chaney
had lived in good health (he was 47 when he
died), he would have dominated Universal's
horror period. *Frankenstein* was scheduled to
follow *Dracula*, and the actor had a sufficient
name to make them both commercial successes.
But it is open to question whether Chaney
could finally have excelled at either part. He

Leone, the vampire's victim in Dreyer's *Vampyr*, is played by Sybille Schmitz, a disciple of Max Reinhardt and one of the few professional actresses in the film.

her father. But the rest of the cast was entirely non-professional, chosen by Dreyer in shops and restaurants for their appearance and external mannerisms.

After weird pulsating credits the film begins with David Gray's arrival at a secluded inn. The titles tell us that 'There exist certain beings whose very lives seem bound by invisible chains to the supernatural . . . their imagination is so developed that their vision reaches beyond that of most men. David Gray's personality was thus mysterious.' And the film proceeds to develop this point almost immediately. For Gray's night at the inn initiates an almost religious atmosphere of the proximity of evil: the camera tracks along oppressive corridors, shapes appear fleetingly from the upper landings. Finally an old man carefully enters his room repeating, 'She must not die.' And after

a pause he gives David a parcel to be opened in the event of his death.

Outside the hero's second sight can make out strange prancing shadows in the sunlight. He follows one and comes upon a deserted building with more shadows dancing. Later he sees a snowy-haired wrinkled old woman and watches her being handed some poison by the village doctor. At a nearby château, David then discovers the old man he had seen in his room the previous evening. It transpires that he owns the château and his older daughter Leone is the victim of an inexplicable malady. A mysterious shot kills the old man and, when Gray opens the book as instructed, he discovers that it is a historical study of vampirism. Gradually, it becomes clear that the old woman is a vampire who is being aided in her attacks on Leone by the doctor. Gray is persuaded to give some of

his blood by transfusion, and in a weakened state he falls into a semi-trance during which he sees the vampire at work and endures a nightmarish hallucination of his own burial. When he wakes up, an old servant has found the vampire's tomb and together they stake her. This purges the infection in the village, and the doctor is suffocated in a cage of a flour mill, as David and the chatelain's younger daughter walk away into sunlight.

Dreyer achieved an atmosphere of miasmic horror by the way in which he photographed this sporadically mundane story. In interviews, the director tells how he secured the grey twilight effect by directing an artificial light through a gauze onto the camera. Moreover, the land on which the château was situated had ponds and lakes, with an abundance of natural mist and Dreyer used to insist on shooting at dawn every day to give the best illusion of dusk. The crew would rise at 4 a.m. and if they missed the correct light, shooting was delayed until the following morning.

The strangeness of *Vampyr* also derives from the way it is constructed as a hermetic ritual, from which the central character is continually and rigorously excluded. He is like an author surrounded by the phantoms of his own imagination, wandering through the proceedings in curiously formal and discreet modern clothes which immediately separate him from the other characters. Nothing he does or says seems to have any great effect on them, and significantly his most direct involvement (the burial) turns out to be a trance. Even the final staking of the vampire is initiated and conducted by the servant at the castle with Gray in the role of assistant. This technique might in other circumstances have amounted to a distancing device, but here it greatly contributes to the plot's engulfing strangeness: the very fact that the hero seems to have no real relation of any definable kind to what is actually happening only serves to make the total effect more dislocating.

Vampyr was not destined to have any immediate impact on the history of horror movies. Its sombre, disorientating beauty proved difficult for audiences and it never achieved wide commercial distribution. But fortunately it is the kind of film that never disappears completely, so that its influence has permeated subtly but distinctly through to a number of directors, perhaps most noticeably in black magic pictures like Sidney Hayers' excellent *Night of the Eagle* (US title: *Burn Witch, Burn*). Its influence on the vampire movie as such is negligible, although there is one drawn-out shot of the vampire's victim fighting the sickness in her soul, which prefigures the later sexual preoccupations of the genre. Otherwise, Dreyer's delineation of the undead as an ancient crone has very rarely featured in movies, except by means of the miraculous last-reel transformation.

THE UNIVERSAL VAMPIRE

'A tall, thin man, clad in black'

Bela Lugosi, as he appears in the first major American vampire film, Universal's *Dracula*.

A typically theatrical pose for Bela Lugosi and Helen Chandler as Mina in Tod Browning's *Dracula*.

IN 1930 AS IT prepared to unleash the 'horror' film on the American public, Universal Pictures was in a distinctly anomalous position as a 'major' American film-producing organization. Smaller than the 'vertically integrated' companies who owned vast numbers of their own theatres, Universal existed somewhere in between the golden heights of Metro/Paramount/Warner and the depths of Poverty Row like Tiffany and Majestic (two early 'B' companies, both out of business by 1935).

But the company was fortunate to have as its founder and reigning monarch a shrewd and energetic German immigrant called Carl Laemmle. Laemmle had arrived in America in 1884 and soon became the manager of a clothing store in Wisconsin. A few years later he hired a vacant room on the west side of Chicago that was usable as a 'picture show'. A punctilious little man, his polite and scrupulously clean booth quickly attracted customers and in no time at all it was part of a chain. After Laemmle had formed his production arm IMP he was one of the very first to see the possibilities of the star system and managed to steal Mary Pickford from Biograph by offering her double wages. He capitalized on this investment by revealing her name on the screen for the first time.

In 1912 Laemmle formed the Universal Picture Corporation by amalgamating his own Independent Motion Pictures with the Universal Film Company of Patrick Powers. The usual internecine disputes between upper management followed, but Laemmle finally emerged as the sole ruler of the new establishment and consolidated his position by the move to Universal City, a multi-acred chicken ranch in the then under-developed San Fernando Valley. From this stronghold Laemmle and his son produced a steady diet of middle-to-low budget westerns and comedies, crowning his crop each year with two larger prestige productions which acted as window-dressing for the more routine material. He just survived the era of intensive studio competition known as the 'bankroll war' by allying himself with an investment banker in 1925 and purchasing several hundred cinemas in minor cities. This in no way compared with the vast circuits ruled by Paramount, Loew or Fox but it did give Universal a safe hold in the smaller theatres, on which it relied for the distribution of its low-cost productions.

Laemmle's move had temporarily consolidated Universal's middling position but the studio was hit harder than most by the advent of sound. Only the enormously successful prestige production of *All Quiet on the Western Front*, which won the company's first Academy Award in 1930, really put it back on the rails. And as the modern era got underway, the Laemmles were fronting a curious hybrid of an organization which was neither a top-flight major studio nor a quickies factory. The company's marginal status and Laemmle's German background make the pioneering excursion into Gothic horror more understandable. It also to some extent determined the form it would take: like Universal itself, *Dracula* is a strangely hybrid creation, something between a prestige production and a programmer. There is evidence that much of its shooting was rushed and even by the standards of the time its special effects are miserable. But it incorporated aspects which were revolutionary in movie terms, notably its adoption of what Browning had called 'the horrible impossible'.

There is every indication that Universal were undecided about *Dracula* from the beginning. Even after the play had become a big Broadway success in the autumn of 1927, nearly three years had to pass before the studio began active preparations to mount it for the screen. But once things had been set in motion, economy demanded that they move swiftly and *Dracula* was shot in a few weeks in the autumn of 1930 for release the following February. After Chaney's unexpected death various candidates had been considered for the title part, including Conrad Veidt and Ian Keith. Finally it was allocated to the Hungarian actor Bela Lugosi who had been a success as Dracula on stage and had since played in a few films like MGM's *The Thirteenth Chair*, directed by Tod Browning.

Bela Lugosi's career has become one of the great Hollywood mythologies: there are as

many versions of his background and his life-style as there are Lugosi credits (he appeared in around 97 films). Even his date of birth is contentious, though it was probably 1884, making him nearly fifty when *Dracula* was shot. He was brought up in Hungary and arrived in America in 1919. Without the fortunate accident of *Dracula*, Lugosi's chances of success as an American actor in the sound movie era were negligible. His English was so bad that he had only been able to maintain a stage career by learning his parts phonetically, and even in films it is sometimes evident that he can scarcely be aware of the meaning of his lines. But what was a severe handicap in any other acting field became a telling trademark in horror movies, suggesting a demonic alien quality which suited the subject-matter. Using his broken east European accent to elongate every venomous syllable in *Dracula*, Lugosi was able to emphasize how different the part was from anything else the American movie public had previously been offered.

In their publicity campaign (*The Strangest Love Story of All*), the studio did its best to draw attention to this difference. Unlike all the other immoral seducers of Hollywood, Dracula was

Castle Dracula, Universal City, with Lugosi displaying the cloak in which he was eventually to be buried.

a sexual monster with no possibility of redemption: no heroine could tame him. And of course he ran the serious risk of causing a moral outcry. This was one reason why it was necessary to pull so many of the film's punches. Most of the plot's real drama takes place off-screen and is transmitted to the audience in one of the long and tedious stretches of filmed dialogue.

In fact, most of what is interesting in Universal's *Dracula* is traceable to its photographer Karl Freund, one of the classic expressionist cameramen from Germany, and a former associate of Murnau. Laemmle had welcomed such talents to Universal and later Freund was to direct Universal's third great horror original *The Mummy*. But Freund's astonishing facility with monochrome is only really evident in the first section of *Dracula*, the section on which the film's reputation rests. It was also the part which won audience attention at the time, containing most of the lines that made Lugosi famous.

Although screenwriter Garrett Fort attempted to go back to Stoker's *Dracula* for his script, as well as the Deane/Balderston play, the scenario he concocted is almost as stagebound as the original Broadway production. Fort was evidently under orders to show as little as possible, with the result that even the Count's death-scene takes place at second hand. But the opening does at least resemble Stoker to some degree: Renfield (temporarily taking over Harker's function in the novel) arrives at a remote Transylvanian village where the inhabitants are terrified to hear he is awaiting a coach which will take him through Borgo Pass to Count Dracula. The mysterious coach arrives and carries him on a frantic, precipitous run along perilous mountain roads, and when Renfield attempts to shout at the driver, he can only see the shape of a bat suspended over the coach. At last he catches sight of a tall hilltop with the peaks of Castle Dracula. The whole sequence of this journey is handled rather well, considering the paucity of resources.

Renfield proceeds through creaking doors to a vast cobwebbed mausoleum, which seems to be utterly ruined and deserted, until a black-caped figure bearing a candelabra looms at the

top of the stairs and proceeds to utter the most famous single line in horror movies: 'I-am-Dracula. I bid you-*welcome.*' The line is spoken in a slow exaggerated drawl, with about as much foreign menace as it is possible to conceive. Later, in case the point is not taken, the Count passes magically through a spider's web on the stairs and turns grimly to his guest: 'A *spider* spinning its web for the *unwary fly.*' Upstairs, in more comfortable surroundings, Renfield proceeds unhappily to business and, when he cuts his finger, the Count is ready to attack him then and there, but is temporarily arrested by the crucifix around his neck. Later, while administering hospitality, the Count observes with a leering half-smile: 'I never drink-eh-*wine.*' And then departs with the unmistakably contemptuous 'Goodnight *Mister* Renfield', again spoken with a huge pause between each word and a fair one between each syllable. The wine is drugged and Harker falls to the floor, whereupon Dracula's

three brides rush in. Renfield becomes the Count's slave and the vampire can effect a speedy departure for England.

The visual quality of much of this is outstanding, although it is sometimes difficult to appreciate on television or in grainy modern prints. But even here, in what is *Dracula's* most telling sequence, Freund's brilliance is continually undercut by Browning.

If there is one adjective that describes the director's handling of the Count it is 'grotesque'. The visual and aural emphasis that he insists on attributing to Lugosi's every word pushes the character to the most extravagant shores of theatrical melodrama. Consider by comparison Stoker's own introduction of the Count motioning 'with a courtly gesture', grasping Harker's hand and saying, 'Welcome to my house. Come freely. Go safely. And leave something of the happiness you bring!' which he follows with an even friendlier: 'The night air is chill and you must need to eat and rest.'

Mina (Helen Chandler) in a semi-hypnotic trance is carried off by Dracula.

ishness from the first time he opens his mouth. He is a thug, and as such his capacity to threaten is drastically limited.

This does not mean, of course, that Lugosi did not exude a memorable and venomous power as a screen presence. His greatest gift as a performer was his energy. He would channel the same excessive intensity of evil into every role he played. And the results were always the same: highly distinctive yet quite one-dimensional. There is something sadly inevitable about his career subsequent to *Dracula*. His decline into a living screen caricature, and finally even a stooge for such comedians as Abbott and Costello (*Meet Frankenstein*, 1948) and Arthur Lucan (*Old Mother Riley Meets the Vampire*, 1952), has been the subject of much lament, but really it is difficult to see his screen persona heading any other way. Lugosi's Dracula-style left no room for development. A sexual element was implicit, as is indicated by the actor's subsequent fanmail from women and his own previous career as a romantic lead, but it was a heavy-handed and superficial sexuality, given more credibility by the vampiric associations of the film than it actually deserved. Consequently there was no direction it could take except that of self-parody. Lugosi often protested that he was trapped by the role. It is hard to imagine how he would ever have been able to exist as an actor without it. After *Dracula* only a tiny handful of films like the remarkable *White Zombie* really benefit from his presence. In his native country he could have achieved a success (though Lugosi's own claim that he was a matinée idol in Budapest has never been substantiated), but in the American cinema his florid approach was technically out of place by the late twenties, and his difficulties with English limited him still further.

Unlike Karloff, who had all the range of a modern actor, Lugosi was frozen in a striking bravura posture, the living tableau of a silent stage actor trapped in modern sound movies. It is precisely because Lugosi was an

American poster for one of the more comprehensive of all the Universal monster rallies, *Abbott and Costello Meet Frankenstein*.

Harker even adds that 'the light and warmth of the Count's courteous welcome seemed to have dissipated all my doubts and fears.' The difference is fundamental.

The fact is that Stoker was well aware of the danger of making Count Dracula into a ludicrous and stagey caricature, but Browning and Lugosi were not. The Dracula they invoked is simply a cardboard villain who, by virtue of the new technical resources of the cinema and Lugosi's unusual qualities as a personality, was able to make an enormous impact on the picture-going public. But in doing so, he sacrificed the one quality which Stoker had consciously or unconsciously sweated to instil into his creation: the quality of ambiguity. Because Count Dracula in the novel is a charming, intelligent and fascinating host, he poses a real moral and sexual threat to the community he is bent on destroying. But Lugosi's *Dracula* announces his glowering brut-

The bastardization of Universal's monster themes: Lon Chaney as the Wolfman menaces Bud Abbott in *Abbott and Costello Meet Frankenstein.*

anachronism, allowed to flourish by an accident of genre history, that he exercises such a fascination, even at this distance. His exaggerated gestures and diction stand out with a dazzling clarity from the pale and more modern shadows with which he was surrounded, making that looming malevolent shape into the ultimate stereotype of all heavies. As a personality, as a phenomenon, as a star, he was remarkable. As an influence on the emergent horror film, struggling for freedom from stage melodrama, he was disastrous.

The public success of *Dracula* was immediate, but it was quickly overshadowed by Universal's immensely superior *Frankenstein* the following year, which had the benefit of much better critical notices than its predecessor. A rough title check shows that while Universal found it profitable to use Frankenstein's name in the title of no less than six further features up to 1948, in the same period Dracula was on the

hoardings of only half that number (years later Hammer and Christopher Lee were to reverse this priority). Universal's *Dracula* had started the first of the two great cinematic horror booms, but it was *Frankenstein* that became *the* Universal monster. In fact, despite the success of *Dracula*, it never seems as though the studio was all that easy with the vampire theme. The more successful Universal monsters were almost always sympathetic creatures trapped by their own destiny. The mummy, the werewolf, and especially Frankenstein have a human and noble quality that the vampire generally lacks. This may explain those quite ludicrous moments when the studio tried to wrench Count Dracula into their own conception of monsterdom. The unforgivable point in Browning's *Dracula*, where the Count is heard muttering 'To die, to be really dead, that must be glorious . . .' (fortunately reduced to insignificance by Lugosi's unswervingly evil performance),

Boris Karloff threatens an emasculated Count Dracula, played by John Carradine, in the first Universal monster rally, *House of Frankenstein*.

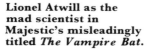

Lionel Atwill as the mad scientist in Majestic's misleadingly titled *The Vampire Bat*.

was taken to its final inane extreme in later movies like *House of Dracula*, where Dracula is presented as some kind of metaphysical invalid, seeking cure for his afflictions.

But in fairness to Universal, other Hollywood studios seemed equally reluctant to grasp the vampire nettle. Amongst several basically counterfeit vampire movies that mushroomed after *Dracula* was Majestic's *The Vampire Bat* (1933), a static Lionel Atwill thriller where the vampire is only a mad scientist requiring blood for his experiments, Invincible's *Condemned To Live* (1935), in which the vampire turns out to be a werewolf and even Browning's *Mark of the Vampire* for MGM, which indicated the director's continuing dislike for truly supernatural material. The film is another reflection of his old Silent Era avowal not to

ask audiences to believe 'the horrible impossible'.

Mark of the Vampire was a straight remake of *London After Midnight* and its vampires, including Lugosi, are subjected to the same undignified rational explanation at the film's conclusion: they are actors hired by a police inspector to catch the murderer. This anodyne ending perhaps led Browning to inject a little more supernatural vigour into the creatures themselves and, with the help of superb photography from James Wong Howe, the vampires achieve a level of conviction (including even one suggestive snarling from Carol Borland) which he never allowed Lugosi's *Dracula*. But the rest of the film is concerned with static exposition, and Lugosi himself, perhaps fortunately, has very little screen time.

It was not until 1936 that Universal got around to mounting some kind of sequel to *Dracula* and at the same time, by sleight of hand, the studio managed to eliminate the Count altogether: in *Dracula's Daughter*, written like its predecessor by Garrett Fort, Gloria Holt plays Countess Maria who arrives to claim her father's body and then proceeds to burn it in an attempt to rid herself of the family curse. Edward Van Sloan is back as Van Helsing but his opponent here proves reluctant in the extreme, even at one stage consulting a psychiatrist for a cure.

Although frequently insipid in the movies, this capacity of the female vampire to struggle against her affliction lacks the ludicrousness of its male equivalent because it has such a strong literary base both in Le Fanu's *Carmilla* and

even Stoker's *Dracula*. There, Lucy alternates on her death-bed between noble martyr and voracious vampire as her horrified lover looks on. This notion of the schizoid female vampire was later utilized to exemplify and caricature the male polarization of woman into goddess and animal. *Dracula's Daughter* skirts these suggestions, but Holden's hypnotic encounter with a female victim, hired by a servant to pose for her, had a suppressed quality of lesbian eroticism that hints at the fleshy delights that lay in store for her successors.

Carl Laemmle and his son had been ousted from the management of Universal in the year that *Dracula's Daughter* was made, and the studio was taken over by two Americans, J. Cheever Cowdin and Nate Blumberg, with some British financiers. As the thirties ended

The carnival exhibition of mad scientist Boris Karloff in *House of Frankenstein*: one of the chief attractions is Count Dracula's skeleton.

Below and opposite:
**Carol Borland and Bela
Lugosi as the imitation
vampires in Brown-
ing's remake of** *London
After Midnight,* **Mark
of the Vampire**.

and the war years began, Universal's production policy became narrow in the extreme and
their dependence on Abbott and Costello,
Francis the Talking Mule and others would
lead eventually to an enforced amalgamation
with International in 1946.

In the meantime, the horror repertoire was
inevitably dragooned into service to drum up
revenue, and the demeaning process began via
Frankenstein Meets the Wolfman in 1943, with
Lugosi shambling pitifully through the part of
Frankenstein's monster. Columbia got the
general idea and made their own Dracula-
meets-the-Wolfman called *Return of the Vampire*
the following year, but director Lew Landers,
who had until then been mainly concerned
with churning out war features, gave the idea
some nice twists. Set in wartime London,
Lugosi played a long-dead vampire called
Armand Tesla, revived when a blitz bomb
unearths his coffin and some workmen remove
the stake, in the belief that it is shrapnel.
Unfortunately, once Lugosi is joined by a
reluctant werewolf assistant, the proceedings
deteriorate. But the minor success of these two
films more or less suggested it was possible to
run the horror characters into the ground and
still produce some audience response.

Very soon afterwards Universal began to
utilize Dracula as little more than a guest
turn to beef up vapid plots. But, before letting
go completely, the studio still had some hope of
grooming Lon Chaney's son to join their
flagging roster of genre stars. Chaney Jr. had
not originally intended to cash in on his father's
success but, after being forced out of work by
the depression, he had entered movies in 1932
and finally made a name with *Of Mice and Men*
in 1939. By 1943 Universal had starred him as
the Mummy, the Wolf Man and Frankenstein's
monster. The studio was still blind to the
enormous division that separated those parts
from Count Dracula, so in 1943 they decided
to build *Son of Dracula* around Chaney as well.

The results should have been disastrous.
Chaney was overweight and podgy-faced, with

Above and opposite:
**Lon Chaney Jr.
appeared in the role of
Dracula, which death
had prevented his
father from playing.
In *Son of Dracula*, the
vampire confronts a
small southern com-
munity and there
marries Louise All-
britton, who plays the
daughter of a planta-
tion owner.**

an acting style that had only just been service-
able in the other monster parts. But fortunately
Universal was still serving as a home for
German talent, now on the run from Hitler,
and *Son of Dracula* benefited enormously from
the collaboration of the Siodmak brothers,
Curt as screenwriter and Robert as director.

Robert Siodmak had had his apprenticeship
in the German theatre and made his Berlin film
debut with the celebrated *People on Sunday*
before becoming a contract director for UFA.
When he reached Hollywood he was able to
utilize his highly developed expressionist style
on a number of thrillers, from *Phantom Lady* and
The Spiral Staircase to *Cry of the City*. Like so
many of the best German émigrés, Siodmak
tried to bring something to every project he
was assigned and *Son of Dracula* was no exception. It was one of the times when Universal's
German connection, pioneered by the
Laemmles, was able to produce something out
of virtually nothing.

For the first time, in Siodmak's film,
Dracula is given a measure of real cinematic
animation and the plot is not uninteresting.
The Count has come to America in search of
blood and battens onto an aristocratic southern
family, then confronting the daughter of the

house. In a major break with the traditions of
the thirties she eagerly embraces the immortality Dracula offers. There are some effective
visual sequences, like the much-quoted night
resurrection, in which Dracula's coffin rises
up from a swamp and mist billows out of it to
metamorphose into the vampire. But even
more interesting is the potential decadence of
Siodmak's theme. For probably the only time
in screen history the victim is less interested by
the Count himself than by the actual prospect
of becoming a vampire. It is a neat inversion of
almost every literary and mythical source, and
it also gave Siodmak the added advantage of
not having to make Chaney too sexually
seductive. But Chaney did his best in the part,
and the results were reasonable. There was
much worse to come.

Universal's monster marathons began in 1944
and petered out five films and a decade later
with the spoof *Abbott and Costello Meet the
Mummy*. Theoretically the idea of combining
all the great Universal monsters at once, which
was the original basis of the series, could at
least have been an exercise in synoptic ingenuity. A few vague elements in Curt Siodmak's
original story-line for the first *House of Frankenstein* (1944) reflect this. But the studio had
neither the time nor the resources to effect a
proper script construction. Their answer was
simply to tailor the monsters to fit the scripts.
So it is that in the first one Dracula is peremp-
torily incarnated to become the miserable
short-lived colleague of a fanatical scientist;
in the second (*House of Dracula*) he is willingly
subjected to a chemical cure that backfires; and
in the third (played by Lugosi for what had to
be the last curtain call) he actually comes full
circle and plans the regeneration of the Frankenstein monster himself. By this time (*Abbott
and Costello Meet Frankenstein* of 1948, shown in
Britain as *Abbott and Costello Meet the Ghosts*),
there was really nothing to connect him with
Stoker's character, except the name and a
passing interest in other people's blood. As the
fifties dawned few people lamented his disappearance from the movie screens.

In any case the era that had begun with the
dropping of the first nuclear bombs on Hiro-

shima and Nagasaki did not seem to favour
the promotion of Gothic superstition. With
limited foresight, Universal had set their
vampire movies in the present, and avoided
the obvious pitfalls only by confining their plots
to a very limited milieu. In *Son of Dracula* for
example the action had been restricted to a
tiny Southern town in the swamp country. Now,
with the horrifying facts of the nuclear age
saturating the American mass-media, the
destructive capacity of a dinner-suited east
European aristocrat could only seem patently
feeble. Instead it was atomic energy that nurtured a new cycle of horror films, as the
American public thrilled to the massive destruction of urban civilization at the hands of a whole
breed of monsters unleashed by radiation,
beginning with *The Beast From 20,000 Fathoms*
in 1953.

The Beast inaugurated what was later to
become known as the science-fiction boom, but
in reality it was less related to written science
fiction than the suppressed hysteria and anxiety
surrounding the Cold War. The great therapeutic advantage of these films was that they
enabled western audiences to enjoy the total
mobilization of the American military without
invoking any of the moral complexity of war.
At the same time their effect remained indefin-
ably disturbing, and it was during the fifties
that producers realized for the first time the
degree to which film audiences really wanted
to be shocked and frightened.

Universal had usually attempted to curb
horrific effects in their films while Val Lewton,
in his occasionally superb RKO horror pictures of the forties, insisted, to the point of
boredom, on the need for restraint. But now
people were flocking to films which relied more
insistently on shock effects than even the output of Monogram and PRC, the old 'B'
factories of the thirties. It was also clear that the
composition of audiences was changing. Television had won the family audience, and movie
attendance was suddenly younger than it had
been. New 'B'-orientated companies sprang up

Count Dracula's only
appearance in *Dracula's
Daughter*. Gloria
Holden, in the title
role, destroys the body
of her father. This
film was the true
sequel to the first Uni-
versal *Dracula*.

Overleaf: **Irving Pichel, as the devoted slave, and Gloria Holden, as the reluctant vampire, in *Dracula's Daughter*.**

The first of the great cinematic monsters freed by atomic energy was *The Beast From 20,000 Fathoms*. It swims to New York after an atomic explosion in the Arctic and follows in Kong's footsteps, devastating the city.

to cater to the new market, and names like American International replaced Republic and Monogram.

Even, so the vampire had never seemed further away: a bloodsucker was the villain of Howard Hawks's remarkable science-fiction movie *The Thing* in 1951, but it turned out to be a highly developed extra-terrestrial whose flying saucer had crashed. Lugosi made a fleeting reappearance in *Old Mother Riley Meets the Vampire* the following year, but the plot of this British travesty only emphasized the credibility gap that now existed. Lugosi played a scientist, the owner of a robot, who deludedly *believes* himself to be a vampire.

Amidst the technological and scientific hardware that flooded the screen, a Gothic revival seemed out of the question. The only possibility for Hollywood screenwriters was the scientific bastardized version that had already filled out plots in the more tiresome 'B' features of the thirties. *The Vampire* of 1957, for example, is a doctor who swallows some 'vampire' pills developed by science and goes on a bloody rampage. *Blood of Dracula* (known more honestly if less commercially in Britain as *Blood Is My Heritage*) gave the same theme a mandatory teenage orientation: a chemistry teacher at a girls' prep school inadvertently transforms a teenage pupil into a blood monster. These films were merely amusing spin-offs from the science-fiction boom. In fact, by 1957 things had reached such a nadir that when a cut-price producer did pump out a listless formula picture called *Return of Dracula*, involving Count Dracula as an illegal immigrant to a small American town, it went by virtually unnoticed. A year earlier Lugosi had died penniless in Hollywood, the victim of a massive heart attack brought on by two decades of morphine addiction. It was the undead's darkest hour.

But, although no-one knew it at the time, science fiction was actually preparing the ground for a new era of vampire cinema, one that would be a good deal more faithful than

A Belgian poster for the saddest of all Lugosi's later attempts at exploiting his screen image, the British *Old Mother Riley Meets the Vampire*.

before to its origins in literature and folklore. The audiences were now readier than ever to face the 'horrible impossible'. Battered by the disturbing and pessimistic connotations of the Cold War horror movie, they yearned for a return to fantasy of a more psychological and less social nature. Censorship was, moreover, imperceptibly weakening, making the introduction of sexual suggestion more feasible. And the onslaught of television made it ever more necessary for the cinema to produce action and spectacle that the small screen could not handle.

In retrospect, all that was really necessary was an answer to the thematic problem that had plagued American attempts at the vampire theme: how could a modern audience, saturated in the material anxieties of the post-war period, respond to what was basically an outmoded superstition? Hammer Films may take exclusive credit for devising the solution, and in doing so they opened Pandora's Box. Dracula, they reasoned, *could* be reborn again, but only amongst the whole gamut of Victorian trappings and inhibitions that had originally given him life. 1957 was, after all, a good year for vampires.

THE BRITISH VAMPIRE

'London... where he might satiate his lust'

Christopher Lee has become totally identified with the role of Dracula in the public imagination. The red contact lenses are now an increasingly familiar appendage to the part, although Lee himself feels that they have been over-used in the Hammer Dracula cycle.

Hammer films began shooting the new *Dracula* (US title: *The Horror of Dracula*) at their tiny Bray studios on the Thames in Buckinghamshire in November of 1957. Their distributor and co-financier was none other than Universal Pictures, who had been left as astonished as every other American major by Hammer's sudden eruption into the international big league with *The Curse of Frankenstein* the previous year.

Formerly a British production company of total obscurity, their gamble that the public might be ready for a new and more graphic wave of Gothic horror had been a sensational success, breaking records across America for the entire summer. By the autumn of 1957 *The Curse of Frankenstein* had inspired an unprecedented deal by which Columbia (and later other distributors) contracted Hammer to make a minimum of three pictures a year, at a time when other British studios and companies were fighting bankruptcy. The final seal was set on Hammer's status in the summer of 1958, when Universal announced that it would be turning over the copyright in its entire library of horror movies for Hammer to remake. It was to prove a total rebirth.

The circumstances that precipitated such a drastic shift in emphasis for a movie genre, and such a strange volte-face by a major American studio (which might reasonably have been expected to cash in on the new vogue itself, considering that the old *Frankenstein* and *Dracula* sets still stood in Universal City) are culturally complex. In a general sense they reflect that peculiar affinity with the Gothic mode that had enabled England to produce all of the great literary archetypes of screen horror in the first place. Universal had always tried to give their work an English feel by employing many English actors and directors, but they could not hope to compete with the atmospheric tone that English landscape could lend these films and they were unwilling (as well as unable) to emulate Hammer's flamboyantly decadent approach, much augmented by the use of colour.

Moreover, Hammer were prepared to devote themselves to screen horror with a single-minded determination that Universal had never conceived possible. They had their own studio, their own key actors and their own house-trained directors and screenwriters. Most important of all perhaps, they had the courage to withstand the incredible stream of moral abuse that was to pour down upon their heads, as soon as they began to resurrect the themes that had until now been so politely bowdlerized for the cinema. The reaction that greeted Hammer's adaptations of English Gothic can interestingly enough be compared line by line if not word for word with the shocked critical reaction that had once greeted the earliest Gothic novelists.

The immediate economic factors that had prompted Hammer to start so wholeheartedly on the production of horror films were closely linked to the fifties boom in science fiction. In 1953 the British Broadcasting Corporation had commissioned Nigel Kneale to write a television series for them called *The Quatermass Experiment*. The story concerned an abortive exploration of space which ends with the sole survivor returning to earth, where he is gradually transformed into a monster. The BBC was hoping to catch some of the audiences currently flocking to the cinemas to see films like *The Thing From Another World*, and they were not disappointed. But Nigel Kneale was no ordinary science-fiction writer: he was a Manxman and he had already written a whole series of short stories which revealed a shrewd and ingenious creative talent, steeped in the mythical traditions of the Celtic fringe. His hero, Professor Bernard Quatermass, was correspondingly much more than just a rocket scientist: in literary ancestry Quatermass was much closer to Van Helsing than to the technically-minded protagonists of H. G. Wells. As a character he has a quasi-mystical orientation that continually brought him up against the naive materialism of the British authorities. This aspect became quite explicit in the third Quatermass adventure (*Quatermass and the Pit*), when, by means of an ingenious science-fiction

Christopher Lee's first majestic appearance as Count Dracula in Terence Fisher's original Hammer production of 1957.

plot, Quatermass was actually permitted to take on all the forces of demonology.

In *The Quatermass Experiment*, the actual material was more mundane, but it was clear from Kneale's handling of the 'monster' that he had the Frankenstein creature somewhere in the back of his mind. It is Quatermass's scientific experiments which are directly responsible for the tragedy that unfolds when the pilot of his rocket ship returns to earth and begins to mutate into a monster. Even the man's name 'Victor' echoes Mary Shelley's novel, and the last scene in which he has become a vast fungus-like mass on the wall of Westminster Abbey, still apparently appealing to Quatermass for help, has a witty and poignant Gothic splendour.

Hammer built on this element when they decided to make a film of *The Quatermass Experiment* (US title: *The Creeping Unknown*) in 1954. It had been a difficult year for the film

The Count greets Harker in *Dracula*.

The seduction of Mina (Melissa Stribling) from *Dracula*.

Dracula, near to his end, in the last film of the original Hammer Dracula cycle, *Taste the Blood of Dracula*.

industry in Britain, and the company obviously hoped that the series' success on television would ensure that the subject was more or less presold. They also brought over Brian Donlevy in order that the venture would have a chance in the American market. And the film was retitled *The Quatermass Xperiment* in order to cash in fully on the expected 'X' for horror certificate, which had been introduced by the British censor when the old 'H' for horror was abolished in 1951.

In the event, the success of *The Quatermass Xperiment* in 1955 exceeded Hammer's wildest expectations and they immediately made plans to embark on more science fiction, beginning with a film called *X the Unknown* in 1956. Like its predecessor this was less of a straight monster movie than an intriguing fusion of Gothic elements and science fantasy. The action is set in the wilds of northern Scotland. In the first encounter with the radioactive monster, two boys creep through the woods past a menacing old tower which they believe to be haunted. Clearly the team that was to produce so much of Hammer's Gothic (executive producer Michael Carreras, producer Anthony Hinds and scriptwriter Jimmy Sangster) were already aware of the possibilities of non-scientific chills. And after utilizing the same 'X'-orientated recipe and spooky settings, it occurred to them later that year that it might be possible to go further.

There were in any case signs that the science-fiction boom was on the wane. And indeed *X The Unknown* was to do marginally less well at the box office than its predecessor. The logical move would be to cut out the science-fiction elements altogether and see if the public would be prepared to take their horror in a more traditional form. In this way they could actually boost the elements that had made *The Quatermass Xperiment* such a success. That was why *The Curse of Frankenstein* started production at Bray on 19 November 1956.

Its writer, Jimmy Sangster, who had worked his way up from Hammer's tea-boy to produc-

"Dracula"

THE NAME STRIKES FEAR AT THE HEART!

HE'LL HOLD YOU IN A GRASP OF SHOCK!

DRACULA

TECHNICOLOR®

PRODUCED BY
ANTHONY HINDS

DIRECTED BY
TERENCE FISHER

tion manager, must take a large share of the credit for the overall style of Hammer's approach to nineteenth-century Gothic. He was a enthusiast of horror fiction, as was producer Anthony Hinds, and Sangster also had an liking for black humour. He was not ashamed to introduce ingredients into his scripts which, by the standards of the late 1950s, were brazen in the extreme. In the first *Frankenstein*, for example, Sangster realized that it would be hopeless to try and emulate the pathos and majesty of the original Universal movie. Instead he turned it into a kind of Oscar Wilde horror tale, concentrating almost exclusively on the dashing and cruel amorality of the Baron himself (Peter Cushing) who is subtly undermining the elegant Victorian drawing-room society by the grisly experiments in his cellar.

This audacious conception might have been a lurid failure, but by an enormous stroke of good fortune Hammer hired a man to direct it who, at that time, was not acquainted with the Gothic style in literature at all. Terence Fisher was in character and personality less like a movie director than an Edwardian country gentleman. Formerly an officer in the Merchant Navy, he had joined the film industry in 1933

and since then had been mainly concerned with the most moralistic of all screen forms, the Gainsborough romance. As a suitable candidate for horror, Fisher would have seemed completely unlikely if he had not been more recently reduced by necessity to working on a series of action pictures for Hammer and other companies. Consequently, with his Gainsborough training, he seemed a reasonable choice for Hammer's new departure, and they were not to regret it. Fisher directed another seventeen horror films for them before his curtain call in 1972.

Hammer situated their version of *Dracula* in 1885, twelve years before the publication of the original novel. It was a crucial decision, and they held to it for most of the series, until their later attempts to update the myth. Fisher's *Dracula* also begins by quite correctly assuming that almost every single person who paid the price of admission would know roughly who and what Count Dracula is. Therefore Harker is not an innocent shipping clerk, but a clandestine vampire hunter, posing as Dracula's librarian.

His diary's commentary punctuates the approach to Castle Dracula as the film begins: 'At last my long journey is drawing to its close . . . What the eventual end will be I cannot foresee . . . but whatever may happen I can rest secure that I have done all in my power to achieve success . . . the castle appeared innocuous enough in the warm afternoon sun and all seemed normal . . . but for one thing . . . There were no birds singing.'

This opening commentary mirrors Hammer's approach to horror: their speciality is the intrusion of the abnormal into the normal and their supernatural material is therefore almost invariably thematically and psychologically subverse. This explains why the company found it necessary to establish the cosy Victorian luxury of their settings in such wrap-around detail, a detail that had never been considered remotely necessary in low-budget horror before. Hammer knew it was

Andrew Keir as Professor Bernard Quatermass (right) examines the fossilized remains of a Martian. Nigel Kneale's crusading SF hero closely resembles vampire-hunter Van Helsing in his unending mystical battle against the forces of evil.

necessary because the primary theme of their movies was precisely the undermining of the atmosphere and décor they so rigorously established. Bernard Robinson, who designed and refurbished set after set for the company, was one of their most crucial creative personnel. He was responsible for the ingeniously economical exterior castle set against which the opening commentary of *Dracula* is framed. The decision to shoot it in sunshine rather than a filter, with the suggestion of underlying disorder ('no birds singing'), is typical of the approach.

The action proceeds to Harker entering Castle Dracula, where he finds a prepared meal and a cordial note from the Count inviting him to dine. Later he encounters a mysterious woman, and then, as she leaves, a menacing shadow appears between pillars at the top of the staircase. We are induced to expect the entrance of a fiend. The shadow glides down the stairs in a prolonged take, merging long-shot and close-up, to reveal, not the grotesque figure that Lugosi portrayed, but on the contrary a crisply charming aristocrat: 'Mr Harker, I am glad that you have arrived safely.' The audience is uncertain how to react, and the ambiguity is precisely as Stoker intended.

les MAITRESSES de DRACULA

(BRIDES OF DRACULA)

en couleurs

avec
PETER CUSHING
FREDA JACKSON
MARTITA HUNT
YVONNE MONLAUR

Mise en scène de TERENCE FISHER
Produit par ANTHONY HINDS

UNIVERS

A French poster for
The Brides of Dracula,
Terence Fisher's
follow-up to the first
Hammer *Dracula*,
although the Count
himself does not
appear.

Count Dracula has at last returned to the tradition in which he was created, the tradition of English Gothic.

Christopher Lee, the actor who was now to replace Lugosi in the popular imagination, was himself an aristocrat of Italian origin and claims to be able to trace his family tree back to the Emperor Charlemagne. His slightly demonic good-looks and tall statuesque physique made him ideal for the role, and after nearly ten years of supporting parts in movies, he put everything he could into it. He was aided by Sangster's script which managed to juxtapose almost all the novel's highlights, without jeopardizing the story's continuity: Dracula's saving of Harker from the vampire women, Harker's encounter with the vampire in his coffin, the slow mental and physical dissolution of Lucy followed by her return from the grave, the grisly staking of Lucy watched with consternation by her loved ones, the imminent contamination of Mina and the final confrontation with the Count. All of these highlights are preserved.

Peter Cushing as Van Helsing exactly duplicated his original's quasi-mystical yet scientific orientation. 'Established,' he tells his primitive recording machine (a further detail that Sangster incorporates to good effect), 'that victims consciously detest being dominated by vampirism, but are unable to relinquish the practice, similar to addiction to drugs.' This established that physical thrill was a central feature of the victim's relationship to the vampire, and Hammer were to build on that aspect for the rest of the series. Even Van Helsing's perennial difficulty in persuading servants to carry out his sick-room instructions (and the consequent entry of the vampire) recurs in this adaptation as well as the gallows humour of the novel's minor characters.

The changes that Sangster made are mainly in the interests of economy: Harker is vampirized early on and staked by Van Helsing, the Count is deprived of his powers of transformation into a bat or a wolf, and his dependence on darkness is exaggerated. In the novel, Dracula had been weakened but not destroyed by sunlight. Taking his cue from Murnau perhaps, Sangster made sunshine into a deadly allergy of the vampire and so added a whole new weapon to the vampire hunter's armoury, alongside the traditional garlic, crucifix and running water.

The action of the narrative switches to northern Europe somewhere in the vicinity of Dracula's castle though, like all of Hammer's nineteenth-century locales, it did in fact resemble a slightly caricatured version of Victorian England. Sangster also redesigned the climax of Mina's illness so that Van Helsing and Holmwood are outside grimly guarding their home from intruders, while Dracula, in his role as the indigenous domestic parasite, is inside rampaging through its women. Finally Van Helsing and the Count stand face to face in the throne room of his own castle and the vampire hunter swings on the drapes to let in the sunlight, reducing his foe to a pile of dust.

Sangster's rigorous stratification of the vampire's code in Hammer's *Dracula* more or less laid down the rules of the genre as they were to be followed by film-makers for the next two decades.

In view of the disgust with which Hammer's *Dracula* was received in some quarters, it is interesting to see in retrospect just how explicit it was. There are three acts of vampirism visible in the film with several more suggested: of the three, one is obscured by Dracula's cloak, one is the sudden bite inflicted on Jonathan by the vampire woman and the third, near its conclusion, has Dracula caressing Mina in close shot and bending down to draw blood: it is the only time we actually witness Dracula's activity in the course of the film, but of course film-goers were unused to seeing fangs, which Universal had strangely never utilized to any great extent. Of the stakings, there are three: the first (Harker and the vampire woman) is done as a shadow against the castle wall, the second (Van Helsing's staking

Edward de Souza
attempting to rescue
his wife from the castle
of the vampires in Don
Sharp's *Kiss of the
Vampire*.

The gruesome resur-
rection ritual which
returned Dracula to the
screen in *Dracula
Prince of Darkness*.

The remorseless puri-
fication of the flesh:
Helen (Barbara Shelley)
is staked in *Dracula
Prince of Darkness*.

Barbara Shelley's new
sexual aggression is
unleashed on Francis
Matthews in *Dracula
Prince of Darkness*.

The reawakened Count
Dracula attacks the
prim Victorian wife
played by Barbara
Shelley in *Dracula
Prince of Darkness*.

of Harker) is faded out before he even picks up
the stake, and the third (the only one we see) is
handled by reaction shots, apart from one
close-up. Interestingly, though, there are two
more physical shots which may have been a
source of distaste at the time: both Lucy's
forehead and Mina's hand are burned by Van
Helsing's crucifix in close shots which graphically evoke the overriding physicality of the
vampire's response. Again, Sangster had taken
this straight out of the novel where a wafer
burns into Lucy's 'flesh as though it had been a
piece of white-hot metal.'

Strangely, the next vampire movie to appear
in Britain was not a Hammer film at all. Jimmy
Sangster's scriptwriting gifts and commercial
acumen were gaining a reputation, and just
after *Dracula* he completed *Blood of the Vampire*
for Robert Baker and Monty Berman. It is an
odd one-off of a film, marking a rare excursion
into vampirism by an independent British
production company other than Hammer, but
it confirmed Sangster's scriptwriting gifts.

Blood of the Vampire is directed by Henry Cass
who subsequently left commercial features
altogether to become a convert of the Moral
Rearmament movement (the anti-permissive
organization which foreshadowed the Festival
of Light). Whether the film had any bearing

on his conversion remains obscure, but it is
certainly one of the most Sadian of the English
Gothic movies. The anaemic greens and reds of
the Eastmancolor process did nothing to
relieve its atmosphere of undiluted cruelty in
the Stoker tradition.

As with so much of Sangster's fifties
Gothic, the film begins with a caption: 'The
most loathsome curse ever to afflict the earth
was that of the vampire, which nourishes itself
on warm living blood . . .' After a brief description of the principle of staking a vampire,
the film opens with a small and solemn crowd
watching a masked strongman hammering a
stake home on a little hilltop grave. But this
opening is quite deceptive, because after a
tavern and laboratory scene, the action moves
to Carlstadt and the wrongful imprisonment of
its doctor hero, John Pierre (Vincent Ball). He
is taken to a vast and gloomy prison for the
criminally insane, the large central compound
of which is given over to floggings, and where
the exterior wall is surrounded by cannibalistic
hounds with spiked collars and the ever-
multiplying graves of the inmates. In this setting
he meets Dr Callistratus (Donald Wolfit), a
bulky, hook-nosed governor who walks around
his grisly laboratory dressed in a velvet jacket,
a voluminous cravat and a leather apron
smeared in unnameable secretions. Aided by a
deformed assistant (Victor Maddern), Callistratus is obsessed with classifying every known
species of blood. It soon transpires that he is a
medical, rather than a supernatural vampire,
whose schemes involve the massive utilization
of his patients' internal organs. 'The practical
side of my work distresses you?' he enquires
leeringly of his hapless housekeeper, as he is
about to recruit her for use.

The complicated exposition finally establishes that Callistratus had been staked because of
his bloody experiments, but had developed a
culture which enabled his body to survive. The
plan worked, but the culture created an infection, and constant transfusion was necessary
to keep him alive. By using his prisoners as a

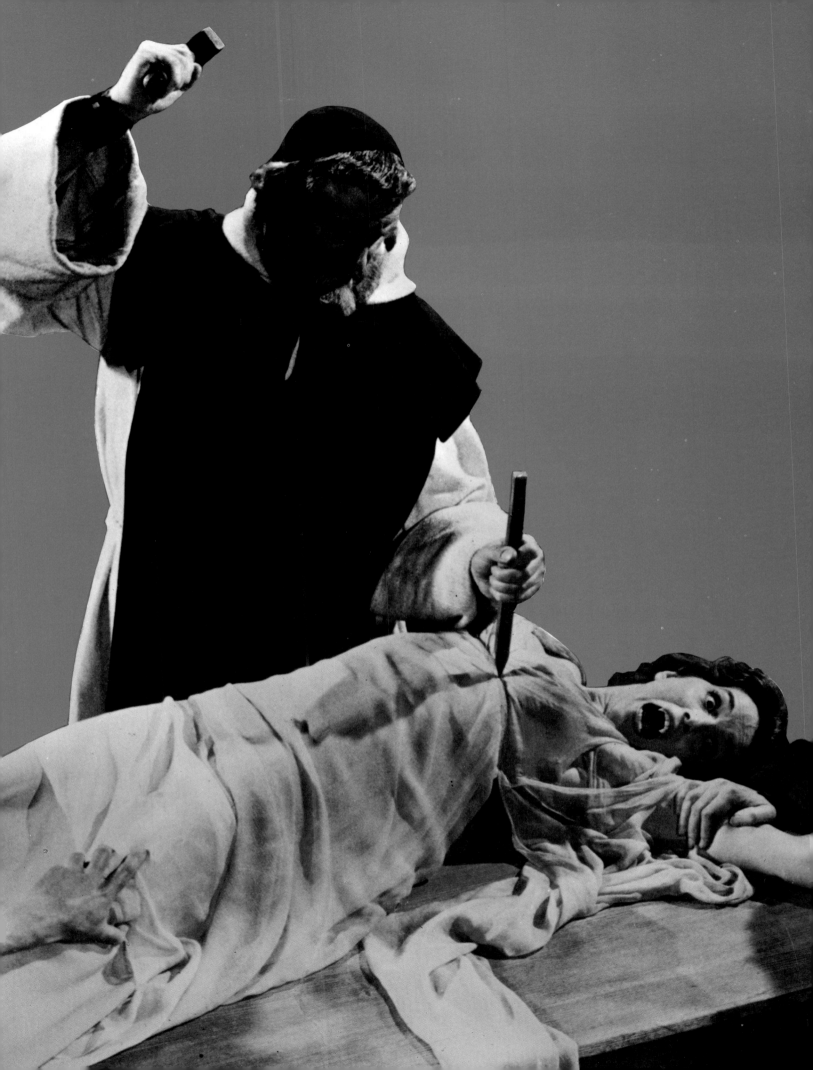

An early victim of the
Dracula cult gratui-
tously incorporated by
director Freddie
Francis at the begin-
ning of *Dracula Has
Risen from the Grave*.

A heretical moment
from *Dracula Has
Risen from the Grave*,
as the impaled Count
wrenches the stake
from his own heart.

Veronica Carlson
lingers over the Count's
coffin in *Dracula Has
Risen from the Grave*.

permanent blood-bank, he was attempting to develop a blood-group which would effect a proper cure.

Almost everything in *Blood of the Vampire*, from the raucous Victorian tavern scenes, and the Dickensian workhouse prison, to the menaced décolleté of Barbara Shelley, is typical of Jimmy Sangster's Victorian under-world, and exactly similar to the tone of his early Frankenstein movies for Hammer. Al-though the action is set in Transylvania in 1874, Callistratus is hardly a Gothic vampire and the film seems to have been made to exploit the success of *Curse of Frankenstein* rather than *Dracula*, which had not actually opened while it was being made (*Dracula* began its run in May 1958, *Blood of the Vampire* opened the following August). But it remains interesting as one of the very few times that a British Gothic movie made a determined effort to merge genres. And with its pre-*Clockwork Orange* theme, it looks forward to the political vampire movies of the sixties. In fact, despite the neatly tailored plot, which allows the hero and heroine a neat escape from what is described in typically apo-calyptic Sangster dialogue as 'an abyss, the bottomless pit of hell itself', *Blood of the Vampire* closely resembles the subversive approach of Alain Jessua's *Traitement de Choc*.

From the fifties onwards, however, Hammer effortlessly dominated the field, although they were acutely aware of the risks of market saturation. This was one of the reasons why they waited three years before producing their second vampire picture in 1960. *The Brides of Dracula* mirrored Universal's own sequel in that it did not feature the Count himself. Not surprisingly this caused serious script problems, which were only resolved by extensive re-writing, and the result is Hammer's only vamp-ire picture with more than one screenwriter credit. Peter Bryan, Jimmy Sangster and Edward Percy battled gamely to avoid anti-climax, and the results were sometimes uneven, though there was greater assurance in handling the myth's paraphernalia.

David Peel plays a sub-Dracula vampire called Baron Meinster who, like so many of the younger Hammer leads to follow him, is afflicted largely by his own decadence. His mother keeps him chained up in her castle (at times the affliction seems to merge oddly with lycanthropy) but a well-meaning visitor sets him free. Among the victims, in an unnervingly incestuous moment, is his own mother who subsequently shows her fangs to Van Helsing. The film is notable for these highly sinister undertones and the reintroduction of Peter Cushing as Van Helsing.

Like Lee, Cushing had been a support-ing actor in films since the forties and had attracted the company's attention when he played the leading part in a television produc-tion of Orwell's *1984*. An elegant, yet somehow soulful screen presence, his original casting as Baron Frankenstein and then Van Helsing was one of Hammer's great coups, and he brought to both parts a remarkable authority, tinged with irony. In the energetic climax of *The Brides of Dracula*, Van Helsing is himself bitten by the vampire, but in a moment of immense masochistic strength he purges the wound with a red hot iron and then utilizes the blades of a windmill to cast the moonlight shadow of a cross which destroys his opponent.

Terence Fisher had directed *The Brides of Dracula* with a similar gusto to the earlier film, and in 1965, he was duly commissioned to mount the Count's official come-back. But before then Hammer made one other vampire film, which fits into no particular cycle. Terence Fisher was away in Germany directing another film, so the company hired Don Sharp to shoot *Kiss of the Vampire*. After the script problems encountered on *The Brides of Dracula*, the producer Anthony Hinds decided to work from his own material, crediting himself John Elder. Elder's name would appear on the majority of Hammer's Gothic movies for years to come.

The script he wrote concerns an English couple, honeymooning in the Carpathians, who are forced to stay the night at a lonely inn.

Overleaf: The land-
scape of the vampire:
Veronica Carlson and
Christopher Lee in
*Dracula Has Risen
from the Grave*.

Alice Hargood (Linda Hayden) lingers over the tomb of her new vampire father, Count Dracula, in *Taste the Blood of Dracula*.

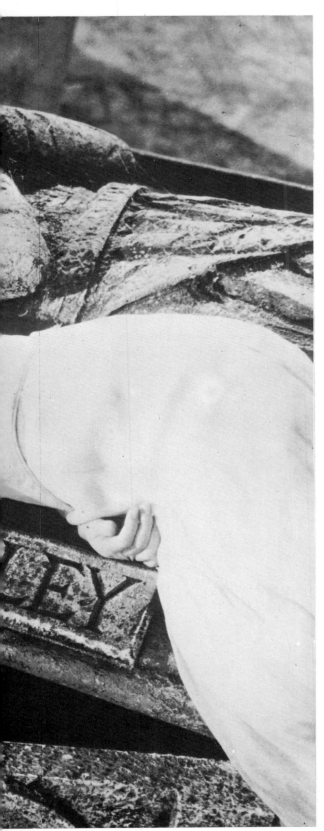

They encounter the charming leader of a vampire cult which closely resembles a black magic coven, and the hero's wife is kidnapped and indoctrinated. The climax of the film concerns his desperate attempt to recover her, aided by the puritanical and gloomy vampire hunter Professor Zimmer (not Peter Cushing but Clifford Evans).

Sharp's *Kiss of the Vampire* is a deftly constructed, occasionally Hitchcockian thriller, which is only marred by an exaggerated performance from the hero Edward de Souza, and the plot's lack of an overall perspective. Isobel Black's venomous energy as a particularly zestful vampire recruit is so splendid that it comes near to unbalancing the whole film. The physical elements of vampirism are handled with a sharp wit, and the use of landscape, notably the lush woodland setting, inaugurates one of Hammer's strongest visual elements. The location (Black Park) was to be used again and again over the years without diminishing in its effectiveness.

The same landscape was a strong feature of the Count's official revival in 1965: *Dracula Prince of Darkness*. At their best, Hammer have always been at pains to maintain the proper chronology, and here they even replayed the last reel of *Dracula* at the film's beginning to ensure that audiences were aware of the proper sequence: 'Here at last,' intones the commentary, 'was an adversary armed with sufficient knowledge of the vampire to destroy him. Thousands had been enslaved by the obscene cult of vampirism. Now the fountainhead himself perished.' The words are spoken like a passage from scripture and, together with the film's title, they set the Biblical tone for what follows. There is also a tease aspect to this

Under the influence of the Count, Alice attacks her human father with a spade in *Taste the Blood of Dracula*.

opening which works on a more elementary level: how are we going to transform this pile of dust back into the title character? The film's enormously protracted opening preamble set about providing an answer.

Two English couples are lost in a forest somewhere in northern Europe and seek refuge in Dracula's castle. They encounter a servant who tells them his master is dead, but has left instructions that visitors should be entertained. That night, after the couples have retired to their rooms, Fisher allows his camera to prowl around the deserted castle in a series of movements which evoke with a poetic grandeur the unseen presence of the departed host. Then the servant lures one of the men down to the cellar where he kills him and utilizes the corpse as the basis of an elaborate ritual to resuscitate his master. The man is strung upside down so that his blood drips onto Dracula's dust and slowly reanimates it.

Even as late as 1965 this sequence could cause a small uproar when the film was released. Fisher intended to depict a full-blown religious ceremony with Dracula as an inverted Christ-figure, and the symbolic crucifixion/resurrection complemented the film's incantatory opening. In fact it was so successful that it left both writer and director with a serious problem: the Count had been revived with a grim seriousness of which even Stoker would have approved, but now that he was established as an awesome supernatural being, there was little that he could do that would not be anticlimactic. Even the smooth ironic charm which had worked so well in the first film, could only appear ridiculous in such a metaphysical context. Consequently the rest of the film was forced to limit Dracula to little more than a background presence. Lee was able to convey a memorable presence in his comparatively brief appearances, but for much of the time he was reduced to the fiery hissing animality of his own victims.

Besides the Count himself, there are a few additional interpolations in *Dracula Prince of Darkness* which are worth noting. The film saw the beginning of John Elder's unsatisfactory policy of ransacking Stoker's book for the odd incidental detail and then mixing it into the action without much regard for context or meaning. In this case the character Renfield makes a belated appearance as a lunatic in a monastery who comes to Dracula's aid. It is a pointless device which does scant justice to the original conception of the lunatic (as an atmospheric correlative for Dracula's gradual infiltration of society) but at least the monastery scenes do contain one impressive sequence. The staking of Helen is handled in vigorous detail that demonstrated at once how much things had changed since Hammer's first *Dracula*. Barbara Shelley never achieved a more perfect incarnation of the demonic physicality of the vampire than in this sequence, where the monks hold down her writhing and screaming body in full view of the camera until they finally manage to pierce her heart. As a precise expressive metaphor for the subjugation of the flesh, the scene remains unequalled.

Dracula Prince of Darkness in fact marked another watershed in the handling of the vampire theme. There has been much speculation as to why Hammer took eight years to mount this grand resurrection, when the first *Dracula* had been so successful. Lee's reluctance to play the role was one factor, but it may not have been decisive. What is generally forgotten is that even after the making of Hammer's first *Dracula*, the British censor remained extremely nervous in his attitude towards the subject. This was not simply a question of cutting the odd close-up.

In 1957, immediately after making *Dracula*, Hammer had bought the rights to Richard Matheson's classic modern vampire novel *I Am Legend*. They even flew the author over to London to write his own script, which was retitled *Night Creatures* and was described by everyone who read it as among the best work of one of America's most talented screenwriters (*Incredible Shrinking Man*, *Fall of the House of Usher*, etc.). But even as shooting was due to

Christopher Lee in
The Scars of Dracula.

The Scars of Dracula :
**Anoushka Hempel
threatens Christopher
Matthews.**

begin word came from the censor's office that, if Hammer went ahead with the film, they could expect an outright ban in Britain. Faced with this pressure, Michael Carreras, who had supervised the project from its inception, had no choice but to pull out. *I Am Legend* has since been remade as *The Last Man on Earth* (1967), with Vincent Price, and *The Omega Man* (1971), with Charlton Heston. Neither version was scripted by Matheson, and neither grasped the paranoid essence of the original. Only three years after this incident the censor slapped a similar all-out ban on the Italian Barbara Steele vampire film *Black Sunday*. Clearly Hammer was having to tread very carefully.

But by the mid-sixties no such care was necessary and sadly Hammer now proceeded to hand over the Dracula series to a succession of younger directors. This meant that the thematic grace and consistency of Fisher's work in the series was lost, although there were a few compensations. *Dracula Has Risen from the Grave* in 1968 was not one of them. The film was interesting mainly because it pointed the overtly sexual path that the vampire movie would now take. It was appropriately retitled *Dracula et les Femmes* in France. The Count's body, frozen in the ice below his castle after the drowning that climaxed *Dracula Prince of Darkness*, is revived by the blood of a cowardly priest who has climbed to exorcise Dracula's castle. The Count, motivated only by an obscure sense of revenge, enlists the priest as his servant and sets out after the Bishop who initiated the exorcism. Finally, after rampaging through the Bishop's loved ones, he is chased back to the castle and falls headlong onto an impaling cross.

The most interesting aspect of John Elder's script on this occasion was the way he builds so determinedly on the religious ironies, beginning with Dracula's priest-henchman and continuing with the atheist hero. He overreaches himself completely, however, with the sequence in which Dracula is actually staked in his coffin but proceeds to pull the stake out of his own bloody heart, apparently because the staking was not carried out with a proper religious conviction. This is really a mockery of the original rules and Christopher Lee has said that he protested against the sequence at the time. The episode carries a temporary *frisson*, but weakens the total effect of the action, because it falsifies the whole fragile structure of the myth on which the film is trying to trade. The same problem has confronted those few film-makers who have attempted (always unsuccessfully and with poor financial returns) to mount vampire spoofs. Even Polanski's *Dance of the Vampires* is finally a good deal less interesting than any of the films it attempts to parody.

But the keynote of *Dracula Has Risen from the Grave* was its overt exploitation of the sexually obsessive aspect of the vampire's victim. Among other things it portrays jealousy for Dracula's favours and a semi-orgasmic reaction to the

Caroline Munro in one of the modish satanic ceremonies from *Dracula A.D. 1972*, the first Hammer film to bring Dracula to modern London.

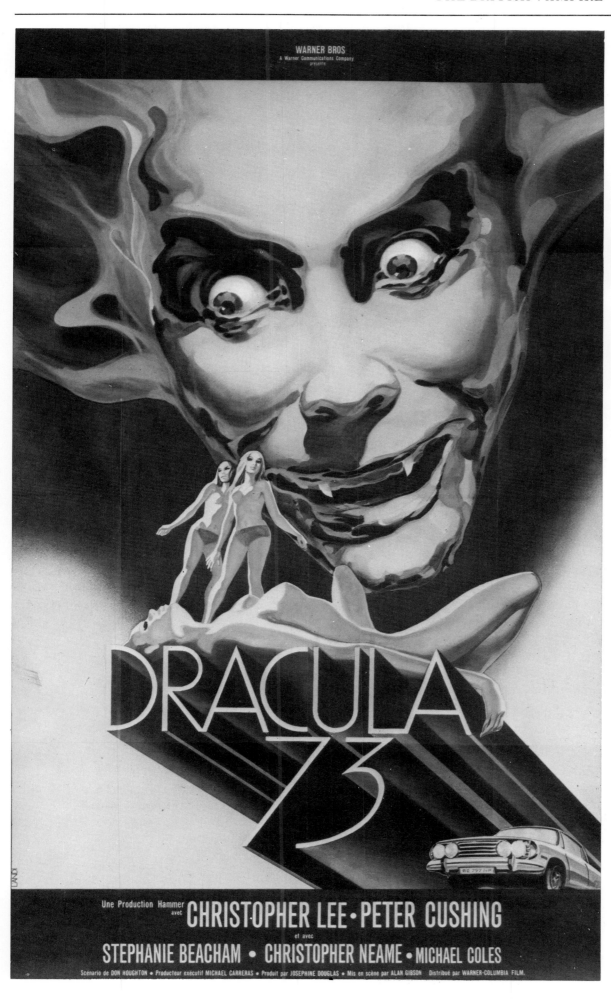

A French poster for the suitably updated *Dracula A.D. 1972.*

Peter Cushing as Stoker's Van Helsing in the opening flash-back sequence of *Dracula A.D. 1972.*

Christopher Neame as the apprentice Dracula in *Dracula A.D. 1972.*

vampire's bite (which would be quite explicit by the next movie in the cycle, *Taste the Blood of Dracula*). A year later Peter Sasdy was to build these new elements into a potentially interesting theme, but here director Freddie Francis (a former cameraman whose interest in the field was purely expedient, as he himself admits) allowed the proceedings to degenerate into a few inconsequential religious and sexual motifs. Only its elegance and Hammer's ever-faithful use of landscape maintain interest. As Gérard Lenne says in *Le Cinéma fantastique et ses mythologies*, probably the most perspicacious book about horror films anyone has written, *Dracula Has Risen from the Grave* is 'a post-critical film, whose naivety is visibly reconstructed.' The freshness and awe of Fisher's approach was conspicuously absent.

But in *Taste the Blood of Dracula*, which is really the last in Hammer's ongoing cycle of sequels to *Dracula*, Peter Sasdy managed to make a virtue of this sophistication. He was aware from the start, as Francis had not been, of the necessity of relating Dracula to his victims by something other than mere plot. And he concocted a film, with John Elder, which was in spirit if not in action almost as close to Bram Stoker's novel as Fisher's last film in the series. This is not to claim that on a basic narrative level *Taste the Blood of Dracula* bears any relation at all to Stoker. Dracula does at last after a particularly fine pre-credits sequence come to Victorian London, but the people he encounters there are all quite new. Where Sasdy captures the underlying strength of the original is in the way he uses the spectre of Dracula to subvert the façade of Victorian society, or more precisely the façade of the Victorian family.

In Stoker's *Dracula* Van Helsing continually alludes to the 'family' orientation of all of those who oppose Dracula. It is a natural metaphor because the Count stands against every Victorian ideal of the family: he is the anti-father and anti-Christ who slaughters babies and procreates laterally by his own sexual perver-

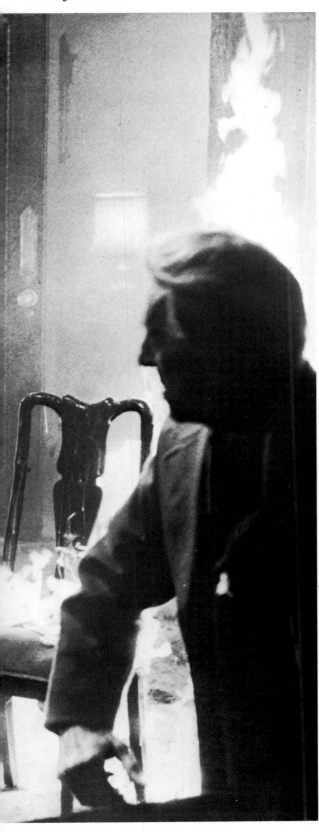

Christopher Lee versus Peter Cushing in the climactic conflagration from *The Satanic Rites of Dracula*.

sion. Sasdy and Elder took this cue from the novel, together with a certain amount of modern theorizing by R. D. Laing and others about the schizophrenogenic family, to make a Dracula movie in which Dracula presides over the disintegration of the nineteenth-century family structure.

With great fidelity to the last film in the cycle (Is there any other genre character who has been resurrected with such scrupulous consistency over a period of twelve years?), the pre-credit sequence of *Taste the Blood of Dracula* establishes that a traveller had watched Dracula's impalement agonies, and scooped up some of his blood as a souvenir, together with his cloak and cane. An apprentice decadent now plans to drink this blood, but he enlists for the ceremony the hypocritical and oppressive patriarchs of three Victorian families. He plays on their boredom, and lures them to an old church, where after a protracted ceremony, Dracula is revived. The fathers have by this time returned to their homes, where they exert a despotic tyranny over their mawkish and passive children who, in this first section of the film, appear quite lifeless and wooden. Sasdy himself describes the impression he wanted to convey as 'bloodless'.

Now Dracula begins to visit the children and unleashes a whole new energy. Under his spell the young take on a vigorous and destructive life: one (Linda Hayden) turns on her father with an axe before languishing with dreamy necrophile abandon over Dracula's coffin. Another slaughters her father and is sucked dry of blood in a sudden (and unexpected) frenzy of the Count's affection/hatred. By the time the hero has extricated the third girl from Dracula's spell, all the fathers are dead and the families decimated. As a chronicle of Dracula's ability to replace the ordered sexual stability of society with a chaotic and dislocating eroticism, the film is disconcertingly consistent.

It proved a fitting climax to Hammer's Dracula series which now regrettably petered out. *The Scars of Dracula* arrived the following

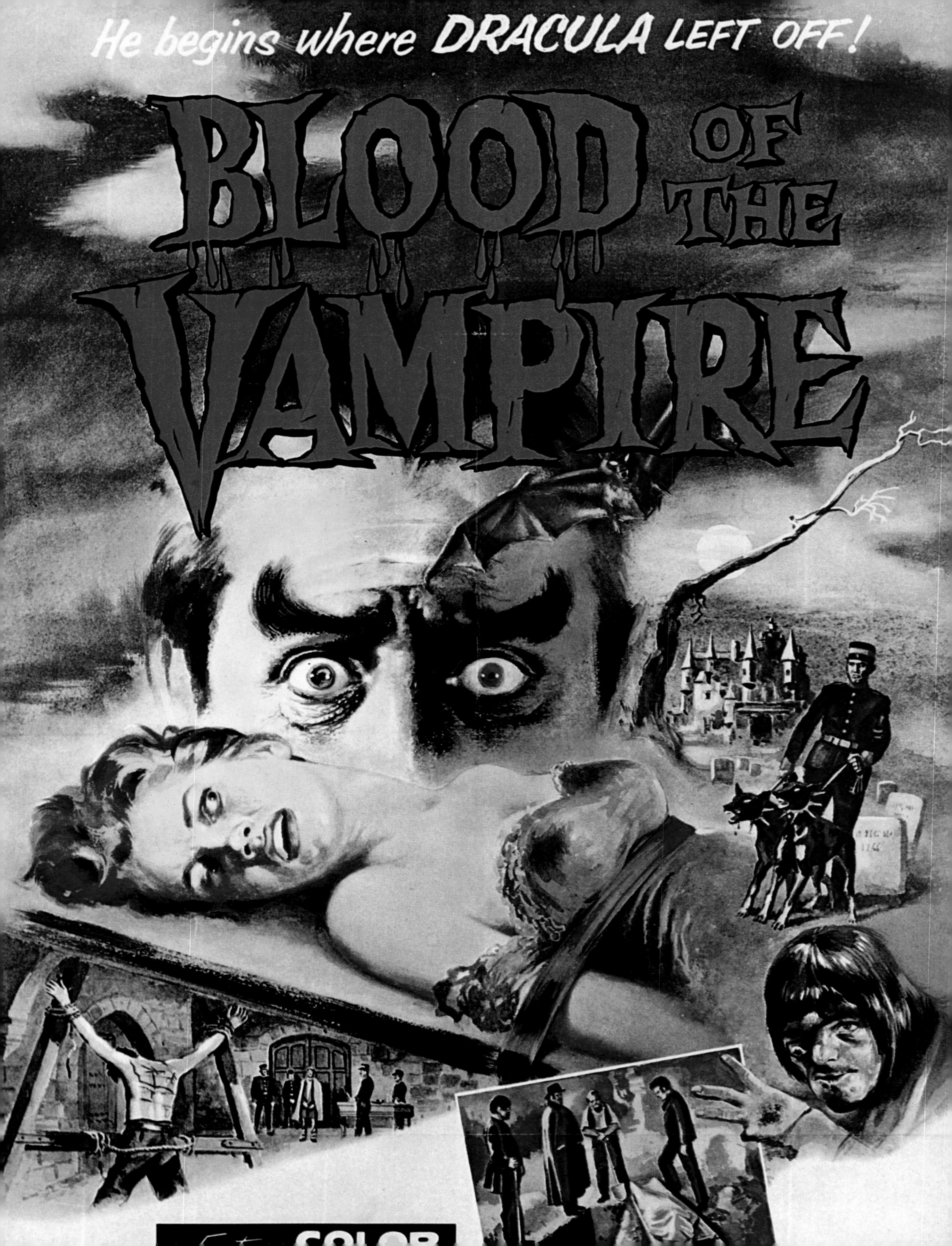
He begins where DRACULA LEFT OFF!
BLOOD OF THE VAMPIRE

**An American poster for
an early British
imitation of the
Hammer style, Henry
Cass's *Blood of the
Vampire*.**

year, making no pretence to be a sequel to the earlier films. At the end of *Taste the Blood*, Dracula had been overcome by the religious ornamentation of a church. In this new film Dracula is apparently revived by a bolt of lightning striking a coffin in an opening sequence which is as ineptly staged as it is incomprehensible. The remaining footage was notable only for an attempt by Elder to return Dracula to his role as an icy, courteous host. But the concession to authenticity was too clumsy and too late. The public had become inured to Dracula as the fearsome all-powerful sexual animal. In the last two films he had been allowed a few lines of dialogue to boost the characterization, but there was really no way that he could suddenly usher a guest into his castle without a far more lucid and imaginative exposition of the situation than was made in this film. And in any case, Elder made nonsense of the whole proposition by adding a lunatic sequence in which the Count is actually seen to stab and whip a victim. Even another belated interpolation from Stoker (this time the Count's crawl down the castle wall) could not come near to saving the film.

As must have been obvious to devotees, *The Scars of Dracula* was the product of a shift in Hammer's management, and their production policy. The company was fast becoming rudderless, and seemed intent on squandering its marketable assets as quickly as possible. *The Scars of Dracula* was released on the same bill as a similarly dire Frankenstein picture, and the commercial results were correspondingly bad. Not surprisingly it was the Count's last Hammer appearance to date in his proper setting unless you count the token guest role in *The Legend of the Seven Golden Vampires*.

Two years later, Hammer reconsidered the Count's destiny in the light of the poor returns on *The Scars of Dracula* and the recent spate of modernist vampire movies from America, like the Count Yorga series. In the circumstances a modern reincarnation seemed a possibility, and Don Houghton, who had now temporarily replaced Anthony Hinds as Hammer's most prolific author, was set to work on a movie with the inevitably eye-catching (yet soon obsolescent) title: *Dracula A.D. 1972.*

Given careful handling, this project could have succeeded, perhaps even inaugurated a new series. By the seventies, the time was right for a modern interpretation of *Dracula*. In fact several impressive short stories had speculated on just this possibility in much the same way as novels like *Rosemary's Baby* managed to reincarnate the devil in modern New York. The Yorga movie series had shown the way and, though they ducked some issues and bordered on parody, their ability to undercut the audience's scepticism, even in a twentieth-century context, was impressive.

For some reason Hammer studiously ignored these lessons and ploughed into the field with a film which invited derision at every possible juncture. It began by pretending to be a sequel to a hypothetical adventure which had taken place in 1872 (always an ominous sign), in which Van Helsing and Dracula engage in a grim death-struggle in a London park. Dracula's ashes are buried in a churchyard, and a hundred years later a demonic teenager called Johnny Alucard (a feeble anagram first employed by Universal in *Son of Dracula*) persuades his gang of teenagers to hold a black magic ceremony in the deconsecrated church where the Count is buried. After most of them have left, Dracula revives and begins claiming his victims. But one of the girls who visited the church is Jessica Van Helsing, who soon alerts the suspicions of her grandfather, a descendant of the original vampire hunter. Meanwhile, without moving from the old church, Dracula succeeds in establishing a little colony of teenage vampires, though his main target is Jessica. Aided by the police, her grandfather succeeds in destroying the vampires, and finally confronts and destroys Dracula in the church.

As will be clear from the synopsis, the makers of *Dracula A.D. 1972* have not even attempted to come to terms with the starting problem of any modern Dracula, which is how to relate the vampire figure to contemporary society. Stoker, in fact, did this marvellously well. His

A French poster for
The Scars of Dracula.

attention of the entire metropolis. The characterization of Dracula had never been feebler than here, with even Lee making heavy weather of the inane situations and dialogue. Peter Cushing struggled manfully to recreate his great role as Van Helsing, but most of the plot's attention was inevitably centred on the young leads, and their mutation into apprentice vampires. Johnny Alucard himself was played by Christopher Neame, an actor tentatively being considered by Hammer as a successor to Christopher Lee.

The fact that Lee no longer wanted to play Dracula and was after fifteen years becoming too old for the role's sexual aspect reveals how much the emphasis had changed since 1931. For even by the early seventies Lee was scarcely older than Lugosi had been in the *original* Universal production. The plan to elevate Neame was in any case scotched, partly because the teenage vampires were rendered ludicrous by the script's incredibly middle-aged attempts at contemporary slang. Only its odd variations on vampire lore ('Garlic is not one hundred per cent reliable,' says Van Helsing at one point) caught the attention.

The same team fared slightly better the following year with *The Satanic Rites of Dracula*, originally known as *Dracula Is Dead and Well and Living in London*. This begins with the summoning of Professor Van Helsing by Inspector Murray of New Scotland Yard after the discovery of a black magic circle involving government ministers. Van Helsing unearths a scientific research centre that seems to be concerned with a mysterious plague virus, and finds a number of girl vampires in its cellar. Concluding that Dracula must be involved, he visits an office block that has been built on the site of the old church where the Count's remains were buried. There, in the film's most imaginative coup, Van Helsing finds that the property millionaire D. D. Denham is Dracula himself, but before he can shoot him with a silver bullet, he is overpowered by the Count's allies, a group of ambitious businessmen. After Van Helsing

Dracula was set in the present and he did everything in his book's opening section to emphasize that this formidable gentleman *was* equipped to deal with legal matters, railway time-tables, etc. His readers were then left to *imagine* the Count's subtle infiltration of London society, and the book proceeds to chart his influence indirectly, with the help of suggestive touches like the lunatic Renfield.

Hammer do exactly the opposite: they bring Dracula to modern London in the first few minutes, but do everything to make it clear that this snarling and anachronistic dandy would be quite incapable of putting one foot outside the church without attracting the

and his grand-daughter, Jessica, have been taken prisoner, one of their party manages to turn the sprinklers on, and in the film's enfeebled climax the Count is impaled on a hawthorn bush.

It was an ignominious and quite illegitimate last exit, but at least the rest of the film marked an improvement on its disastrous predecessor. The best moments suggest how effective a modern transposition of the Dracula myth could be if it were handled with a sufficiently subversive deal. There is even some attempt to situate Dracula in truly contemporary surroundings (What better role for a modern vampire in London than a property specula-

tor?) and to supply him with an original if rather dubious motivation: the destruction of the world and therefore his own death. But the film is betrayed by the tired, computerized sub-*Avengers* style of Alan Gibson's direction and some atrocious interpolations. The silver bullet and hawthorn tree may be forgiven, but even John Elder, at his most excessive, would surely have resisted the temptation to have the Count protected by afghan-clad heavies on motorcycles.

By this point in the history of the horror movie, all real sexual potency and imaginative vitality seemed to have been usurped by the female sex-vampire.

Christopher Lee seduces Barbara Ewing in *Dracula Has Risen from the Grave.*

THE SEX-VAMPIRE

'The ruby of their voluptuous lips'

A graphic act of vampirism from one of Jean Rollin's original and surreal sex-vampire films, *Le Frisson des Vampires*, released in the United Kingdom and the United States as *Sex and the Vampire*.

THE TERM 'SEX-VAMPIRE' is in fact highly paradoxical. As I have suggested in the opening chapters of this book, whether you examine the vampire's origins in literature or folklore or even in the history of psychopathology, it is impossible to divorce the phenomenon from sex. Often the word vampire seems to work almost as a synonym for succubus/incubus, the night demons who were reputed to engage in sexual intercourse with sleeping mortals.

Of course, later, when the vampire became a part of literature, other less overtly erotic factors came into play: suspense, pathos, melodrama, even humour can be found in the novel *Dracula*. But all of them take a very subsidiary role to the sexual threat which underlies the action and generates its particular aura of morbid dread. Universal were forced to moderate this aspect of the book in 1931, but even if they had cast Dale Carnegie in the lead, the subject matter would still have invoked forbidden associations. No matter how hard the film-maker may struggle to abolish sexual content from his vampire movie, it will always return by virtue of the vampire's origins.

Rosemary's Baby is doubly relevant in this context because both as a book and a film it illustrates the peculiar truth that the supernatural *continues* to enjoy a charged sexual connotation, even after psychoanalysis has unmasked it. In his *Structural Approach to the Fantastic* Todorov claims that 'it is no longer necessary to resort to the devil in order to speak of an excessive sexual desire', but for some reason it is still extremely effective. If *Rosemary's Baby* had been readjusted into a humanist frame of reference so that the husband turned out to be not a satanic agent but a callous and treacherous psychopath, it might have worked as a thriller but it would not carry anything like the same sexual charge. Similarly, if any of the sex-vampire movies were rewritten to cut out the whole supernatural slant without removing any of the sexual content, it is doubtful whether they could carry the same weight. The strange truth is that the sexual and supernatural are now inextricably bound up together, culturally, psychologically and historically.

Perhaps in any case the connection between

The typically fetishistic female fantasy figures of Rollin's *La Vampire Nue*, combining a surrealistic, alien quality with the more traditional props of sado-masochism.

Sexuality versus
society: the core of
the vampire cinema;
Yutte Stensgaard as a
lesbian vampire in
Jimmy Sangster's
Lust for a Vampire of
1970. Even in 1970 such
explicitness could only
be passed in the context
of a Gothic horror film.

them is not simply a question of past religious and social taboo, as Susan Sontag has pointed out in *The Pornographic Imagination*. There may well be something about our perception of sex that places it automatically alongside other forms of human fantasy, a transcendental quality that juxtaposes it in the imagination with the supernatural. This might explain why, in the sixties, when film-makers were able to take sex out of the context of 'diabolical temptation' and put it back in the bedroom, the vampire managed to survive.

There is another more prosaic reason for the survival. It becomes obvious as soon as you look at one of the most famous and frequently reproduced stills from *Lust for a Vampire*. It shows Yutte Stensgaard as Carmilla Karnstein sitting up in her coffin in a state of bloody voluptuousness: shreds of drenched and tattered clothing hang ineffectually over her right shoulder, blood drips from both sides of her mouth, forming a little river on her neck which runs down onto both exposed breasts. Now supposing this was not a still from a Gothic fantasy but from a psychological horror movie about a female sadist. Immediately the shot becomes an impossibility. The British censor would only pass it in a film of immense artistic prestige, the American MPAA would either give it an 'X' (which in American terms is the kiss of death for a horror movie; even *The Exorcist* got a more lenient 'R' rating) or ask that the shot be cut to facilitate a less restrictive grading. Clearly in the early 1970s the supernatural was still able to go further than the sex movie, especially in the suggestion of sadistic pleasure.

So really there were two separate reasons for the coming of the sex-vampire movie in the late sixties: on the one hand film-makers were simply capitalizing on the age-old connection between sexual and fantastic themes; on the other, they were utilizing these themes more consciously than ever before to evade the censorship of their respective countries.

The earlier vampire movies nicely avoided all charges of sexual prejudice by dividing their attention equally between the male and female vampire. Universal were admittedly rather timid about the female undead, doubtless because of their erotic connotations, but by the late fifties film-goers were quite used to seeing the animalistic fanged fervour of both sexes, presented as threatening sexual objects. However, with the new sex-vampire movies, attention moved almost exclusively over to the woman, whose gross carnality was depicted with all the lingering and repelled fascination of a medieval cleric. In literal social terms this was of course the most reactionary stereotype available, and to make matters worse it was proliferating at precisely the time when the distorted cultural image of women was coming under deserved criticism. A good many people, perhaps discovering the vampire movie for the first time, attacked it as degrading and sexist.

They have a case, but in general the vampire movie is not concerned with character or realism. The function of the vampire movie is precisely to incarnate the most *hostile* aspects of sexuality in a concrete form. We identify these traits on the screen because they are a part of all of us, rising and falling in their demands like the resurrections and stakings of the vampires. We may lament that this sexual hostility exists at all. But Robert Stoller has asked the relevant question (in a classic paper from the *American Archives of General Psychiatry*, June 1970): 'If hostility could be totally lifted out of sexual excitement there would be no perversions, but would normal sexuality be possible?'

The earliest sex-vampire movies were not so much softcore as surreal. They were the product of those European enthusiasts of the *fantastique* who had been nurtured on the Surrealist-Freudian tradition and who delighted consciously and deliberately in the juxtaposition of erotic and macabre imagery. Up to this point the horror movie had had remarkably little to do with Surrealism except in an instinctive and unselfconscious way, but now in some respects the two forms merged.

Amongst the pioneers of this hybrid was Jean Rollin, who had entered the French film

Les distributeurs associés présentent :

LE FRISSON DES VAMPIRES

UN FILM DE JEAN ROLLIN, PRODUCTION FILMS MODERNES ET FILMS A.B.C

Sandra JULIEN - DOMINIQUE - Nicole NANCEL - Jean-Marie DURAND

Michel DELAHAYE - Jacques RIBIOLLES - MARIE-PIERRE et KUELAN

INTERDIT AUX MOINS DE 18 ANS

EASTMANCOLOR

Some of the surreal
imagery from Rollin's
*Le Frisson des
Vampires*. The poster
was designed by
Rollin's friend, the
comic-strip artist,
Philippe Druillet.

business in 1955 at the age of seventeen as an
assistant director to a small Paris animation
company. After moving on to work as an editor,
he made his first short, *Les Amours Jaunes*,
inspired by the pessimistic nineteenth-century
poet Tristan Corbière, in 1958, just as the
French New Wave of film-makers was coming
to the fore. But Rollin's only association with
the New Wave over the next ten years was an
abortive collaboration with screenwriter Marguerite Duras (who had written *Hiroshima
Mon Amour* for Resnais) on a projected feature
which was never completed.

Rollin did however manage to finance
another short, *Les Pays Loins*, in 1965, by which
time he was making a living in various odd
movie jobs, both as an assistant director and a
sound engineer. Finally an encounter with
producer Sam Selsky led to his first feature, *Le
Viol du Vampire* in 1967, which was programmed
with his short *Les Pays Loins* at various Paris
cinemas in May 1968. Even in those revolutionary times its success was considerable.

Rollin had no academic education, and his
first film reflects a preference for visual effects
rather than narrative continuity, which has
been a feature of all his subsequent work.

Le Viol is a grandiose pulp melodrama whose
half-baked plot, about an attempt to free two
girls from a vampire curse, is really an excuse
for some remarkably audacious imagery and
some wild changes in mood from humour and
suspense to tragedy. *Midi-Minuit Fantastique*
noted that Paris audiences were visibly irritated
by these shifts in tone when the film was shown,
but its popularity was guaranteed by the sexual
ingredients. These included a highly fetishistic
vampire queen who erupts from the sea, and is
later seen in sensual abandon reclining on
the tiger-skin upholstery of her car, young
vampire girls sucking blood from huge bowls,
nuptials in a coffin and a lot of necrophile
suggestion. The film ended with the hero
reciting some lines from Rollin's favourite
author, Gaston Leroux (most famous for
writing *Phantom of the Opera*) to a deserted

Rollin's first major commercial success, *Le Viol du Vampire*, which established the major images and themes of his vampire cycle.

Place de la Bastille, while clutching the corpse of his dead love.

In the context of the French popular cinema in 1968 *Le Viol du Vampire* was a daringly explicit film. Censorship under de Gaulle had been extremely strict, and for ten years English horror had been far more daring and suggestive than its French equivalent (with the exception of a few isolated excursions into the genre by prestigious film-makers like Franju and Vadim). The atmosphere of dreamy sexual excess Rollin created seemed a direct extension of the work of French literary decadents like Théophile Gautier. Two years later Sam Selsky was able to finance a similar production in colour called *La Vampire Nue*.

This was very much the mixture as before, though its tone was a little more restrained and the vampires turned out to be extra-dimensional mutants who planned to take over the earth. Rollin followed it with what was to be his most interesting movie so far, *Le Frisson des Vampires* in 1970. At a superficial glance the plot of *Le Frisson* could be that of any classical vampire horror film from the early sixties: a honeymooning couple Ise and Antoine arrive at their cousins' castle, where they learn that their hosts have died, but are made welcome by two female servants. Gradually, Ise succumbs to the nocturnal advances of a vampire, and they soon discover that the cousins live on as the undead. But the husband is unable to persuade his wife to leave the castle until it is too late.

The plot resembles Sharp's *Kiss of the Vampire*, but the two films are poles apart. With *Le Frisson des Vampires* Rollin excelled himself in the accumulation of erotic imagery, specifically investing the lesbian vampire Isolde with a graphic physical presence that has been rarely equalled in horror movies. She appears on the first night, clothed in lengths of metal chain and leather boots to initiate Ise in a graveyard. Later she takes to manifesting herself Hoffman-like in grandfather clocks and chimneys, always pale and ravenous. In her

LE FIGLIE DI DRACULA

con **PETER CUSHING** e **DENNIS PRICE**
e con **MADELEINE & MARY COLLINSON** · **ISOBEL BLACK**
KATHLEEN BYRON · **DAMIEN THOMAS** · **DAVID WARBECK**
Sceneggiatura di TUDOR GATES · Prodotto da HARRY FINE e MICHAEL STYLE · Regia di JOHN HOUGH
A COLORI   Distribuzione ⓒ CINEMA INTERNATIONAL CORPORATION

Left : **An Italian poster
for Hammer's sex-
vampire film,** *Twins
of Evil.*

Right : **The original
poster for Rollin's
most recent vampire
film,** *Lèvres de Sang.*

final spectacular exit, Isolde is reduced to
sucking the blood from her own veins, a precise and evocative image of the circularity and
futility of physical appetite and excretion.

The rest of the cast is almost equally striking :
the male vampire cousins are exotic hippies
sporting jeans, kaftans and ear-rings and debat-
ing endlessly on the existential predicament
of the vampire, while their servant-girls dress in
diaphanous night-gowns. Much of the castle-
setting is impressively lit and there is a bizarre
beach climax in which the honeymooning wife
is ecstatically reunited with the vampire cousins, only for all three to be destroyed in
conclusive orgasm of pain by the sun's rays.

Although Rollin has made more films
(notably *Requiem pour un Vampire* and *Les
Démoniaques*), *Le Frisson des Vampires* seems to
have been his most commercial work to date,
gaining wide distribution in Europe and
America. Artistically too, *Le Frisson* takes
Rollin's conception of vampirism as a luxuriant
sexual perversion about as far as it can go. On
the strength of it, it is tempting to see him as the
Claude Lelouch of the vampire cinema, a
director who has allowed his undoubted talent
for visual effect to bring him into what is finally
an impasse. All Rollin's films are crammed with
visual extravagance, he is not averse to dupli-
cating the exact details of this or that Surrealist
painting, and Max Ernst seems to be a central
visual influence on his later work. Most of the
imagery is also straightforwardly sado-maso-
chistic, like the spikes that protrude from the
girls' breasts in *La Vampire Nue* or the endless
belts and chains and boots of *Le Frisson*. His
use of colour manages to prevent this from
becoming too repetitive, but by taking the
vampire out of a narrative context and placing
it in an essentially visual frame of reference,
Rollin has deprived the form of much of its
interest. Style and visual virtuosity alone cannot
finally compensate for script construction, as the
career of Stanley Kubrick has indicated.

To prove that the sex-vampire can merge with
a strong narrative, we have Harry Kumel's

Lèvres de Sang

UN FILM DE
JEAN ROLLIN

JEAN LOU PHILIPPE . ANNIE BRIAND
NATHALIE PERREY . PAUL BISCIGLIA
Musique originale: D.W. LEPAUW
Image : J.F. ROBIN

INTERDIT AUX MOINS DE 13 ANS
EASTMANCOLOR

Visa n° 6368

Daughters of Darkness which took up some of Rollin's ideas the following year. Kumel, a Belgian who had worked in television and then taught at the Dutch film school, brought a far more intellectual approach to the subject. Because he was an academic and a movie historian his work is, in the apposite phrase of David Thompson, 'exactly what might emerge from an adventurous course on Gothic cinema and the horror myths coupled with a detailed study of such stylists as Welles and Sternberg.'

Daughters of Darkness begins with a couple, Valérie and Stefan, making love on a modern train as they return from an English honeymoon (the recurrence of the honeymoon as a symbol of sexual vulnerability in horror films is striking). They arrive on the rainy and wind-swept sea-front at Ostend and check into the vast hotel, which – like the town – is completely deserted for the winter. For a while they move through the expanse of dining rooms and lounges in a mesmerizing isolation, surrounded only by a decaying luxury and the fleeting shadows of servants. The sense of aristocratic futility, of a glittering vacuum both in and around them is chillingly conveyed.

Into this lost space as if into a dream, steps the hallucinatory figure of the Countess Bathory incarnated in close-fitting silver lamé, immaculately permed curls and mask-white make-up, as the flawless image of the thirties

Rollin has frequently tended to concentrate on imagery at the expense of the narrative. Certain sequences in *La Vampire Nue* have an expressionist quality which is rarely featured in his work.

The *ménage à quatre* in *Daughters of Darkness. Right and far right bottom :* Countess Bathory's seductive lesbian companion is killed in a shower accident. *Far right top and centre:* Delphine Seyrig, as a reincarnation of Countess Bathory as twenties vamp, manipulates her companion and the young honeymooning couple.

vamp. It is a stroke of enormous luck for Kumel's film that, in order to convey the reincarnation of Bathory from a vicious past, he appeals not to historical but to cinematic memory. Delphine Seyrig as Bathory eschewed the vague unknown horror of a forgotten Carpathian Countess for the half-remembered erotic associations of the twenties and thirties. Yet at the same time, the disciplined erotic greed and appalling *style*, of the cruelty she conveys, is exactly in keeping with the facts of the real Countess Bathory as we know them today from the court records. Later that year Hammer were to make a superficially accurate period reconstruction of the case, yet Sasdy's *Countess Dracula*, despite some points of interest, is far further away from the terrible essence of Bathory's cultural identity than Kumel's film.

The hotel porter is convinced that the Countess stayed there forty years ago exactly as she is now, although her appearance remains unchanged ('Diet and lots of sleep,' she counters later in answer to the same question). Slowly the lesbian Countess, accompanied by a female partner Ilone, begins to enter the lives of the young couple. She excites them with an ecstatic recitation of her ancestor's atrocities and when Valérie, the young wife, is frightened into leaving her husband, the Countess acts as intermediary. Meanwhile her escort has seduced Stefan, but is killed after an ambiguous accident in a shower. The death of the girl ensures that the young couple become even more enmeshed with the Countess and Stefan is finally murdered during their erotic games. Valérie is now completely under the Countess's spell and the two leave the hotel. But when the dawn comes, Valérie is blinded into crashing the car and the Countess is thrown clear to be impaled on a branch.

Unfortunately the traditional ending of the story is not equal to the multitude of ideas and references that have been injected into it, but Kumel nevertheless succeeds in building the first two-thirds of the film into a highly dense and impressive achievement. The

two young girls... trapped
with no escape!
HARRY NOVAK presents
CAGED VIRGINS
Forced
to submit to
the Horrors
of the Pit!
THEIR
INNOCENC
VIOLATED BEYON
DESCRIPTION—
IN AN ENDLESS
NIGHTMARE OF TERRO
EASTMANCOLO

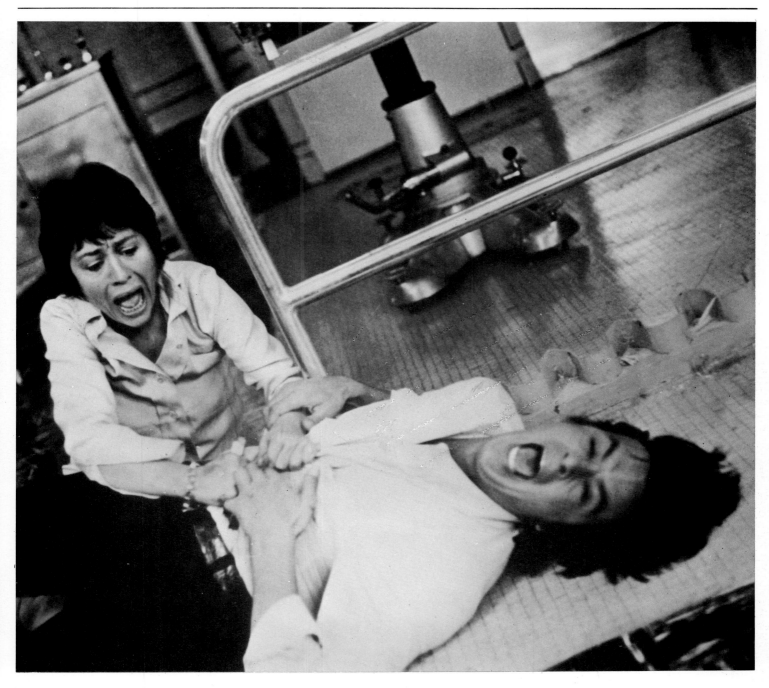

overall framework of ideas is not just sexual but political. The indolence and social alienation of the characters seem to breed the basic perversions on which the Countess is able to play so cunningly. And at every juncture of the film, the brittle elegance of Kumel's décor emphasizes this aspect.

The characters are also allowed a greater emotional complexity than Rollin had ever achieved, making their sexual clutchings more compelling. Rollin had crammed his movies with the external trappings of plot (extra-dimensional vampires, secret passages, ceremonies) but they always ended up with no real narrative development at all, while Kumel utilized the minimum of such devices and yet covered far more ground. This is perhaps why

his gimmick ending comes as such an anti-climax.

The more political implications of *Daughters of Darkness*, especially the Countess's sinister reference to 'diet and lots of sleep', were developed still further by Alain Jessua's remarkable *Traitement de Choc* (1973) (released in Britain under the supremely misleading title *Doctor in the Nude*). This was the story of a luxurious French sanatorium which utilizes the blood of cheap imported Portuguese labour to rejuvenate its wealthy clients. The scene in which Annie Girardot discovers a cannibalized corpse on Alain Delon's operating table and realizes the true contents of the 'special treatment' is vividly effective, as is the last shot of another truckload of victims being herded

Annie Girardot grapples with the new political version of the mad doctor figure (Alain Delon) in Alain Jessua's *Traitement de Choc*.

Opposite: The films of Jean Rollin have been subject to numerous alterations and title changes for foreign distribution: a distributor's press book (opposite) for *Requiem pour un Vampire*, which became *Caged Virgins* or even *Crazed Vampire* on release in the United States.

Imogen Hassall and
Patrick Mower as the
lovers who develop a
taste for vampirism
as a sexual perversion
in *Incense for the
Damned*.

One of the victims of
their blood orgies.

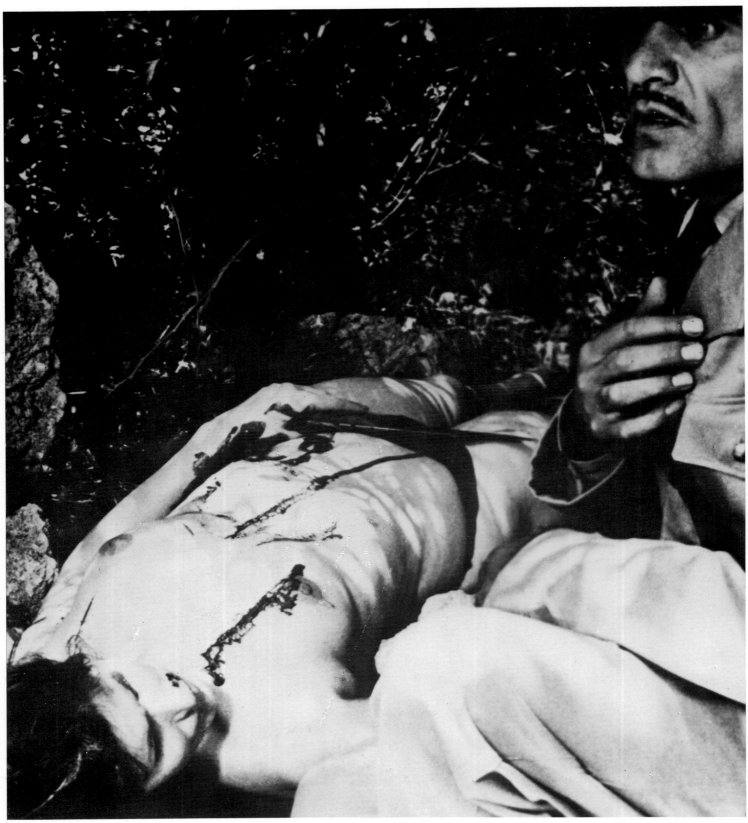

Annette Vadim as Carmilla in Roger Vadim's *Et Mourir de Plaisir* (*Blood and Roses*).

Ingrid Pitt as the age-ing Countess Bathory in Hammer's *Countess Dracula.*

towards the clinic. The 'political' vampire movie (always with strong sexual undertones) has been one of the field's most promising developments, and found its most potent form in America.

The idea of vampirism as a straight sexual perversion minus any supernatural connotations at all was first properly mooted in mainstream fiction by Simon Raven in his novel *Doctors Wear Scarlet* (1959). For a long time the book had been a personal project of director Terence Fisher, but finally a small British company called Titan secured the rights and Robert Hartford-Davis was hired to direct. There were problems during shooting and editing, and Hartford-Davis eventually took legal action. It must be the only time in film history that a director has taken his name off

what easily ranks as his best work, because *Incense For the Damned* made in 1969 stands out from an otherwise undistinguished career.

The film follows Raven's plot extremely closely. A promising young Oxford don, Richard Fountain, who is the son of the British Foreign Secretary, has become involved in the activities of a mysterious group of young people, while he is researching in Greece. His conventional English fiancée and two friends pursue him there through a trail of mysterious deaths and find that he is infatuated by a Greek girl whose sadistic influence over Richard remains unexplained. The psychopathic girl is killed and the Foreign Office and the Greek authorities manage to hush up the affair while Richard is brought back to England.

Meanwhile an expert informs Richard's

Elsa Martinelli confronted by a masked Mel Ferrer in Vadim's film.

friend Seymour that vampirism does exist, not as a supernatural cult, but as a recognized psychoanalytical condition, brought about by acute impotence. The sucking of human blood becomes a substitute for proper sexual activity and gradually engenders a psychological dependence between the impotent man and the woman who allows him to practice it. (This was the nature of Richard's dependence on the Greek girl.) His condition had probably been brought about by the stifling academic atmosphere with which he is surrounded, especially the fact that his fiancée's dominating and ambitious father, Dr. Goodrich, is also the master of the college where he teaches.

Seymour is uneasily aware that the pressure on Richard from Goodrich exists, and his worst fears are realized when Richard's speech at the College Feast becomes a hysterical tirade against the tyrannical bloodsuckers of the academic world, including Goodrich himself. Later, when Penelope goes to Richard's room to comfort him, he sinks his teeth into her throat and later he falls to his death from the college roof. The last (totally incongruous) scene shows Seymour descending to Richard's coffin with a stake.

The best thing about the movie was the way it stuck closely to Raven's central idea that Richard's vampirism was not merely a refined form of sadism but a therapeutic acting out of the stifling parasitic *mental* processes that he feels around him. The theme really needed a Polanski to do it justice, but this approach was quietly effective despite the inexcusable last sequence which made a nonsense of everything that had preceded it. Imogen Hassall made a good prototype of the sex-vampire as Chriseis, the Greek girl, while Madeline Hinde was suitably bloodless as Richard's conventional English fiancée. They never meet in the course of the action, but the implicit contrast between the two girls is in its own blunt way as impressive as the silent dialogue between Wendy Craig and Sarah Miles in *The Servant*.

The moment in which Fountain's friends

Hammer's first sex-vampire movie, *The Vampire Lovers*, was a comparatively faithful adaptation of J. Sheridan Le Fanu's *Carmilla*. Ingrid Pitt, seen centre with Madeleine Smith, plays the oddly sympathetic seductress Carmilla.

enter his Oxford rooms to find that, in a mixture of lust and revenge, he has finally sunk his teeth into his fiancée's throat certainly ranks as one of the more extraordinary images of personal rebellion in the cinema and, as with *Daughters of Darkness*, the sex vampirism it depicts is allowed to benefit from a full symbolic resonance, set up by the script. *Incense For the Damned* had inaugurated the British sex-vampire in 1969, but owing to legal wrangles it was to be three years before the film was released. In the meantime, Hammer had moved into the field, launching their own more fantasy-orientated sex-vampire cycle in 1970. Within the space of twelve months they made three films that roughly fall into this category.

The idea of the Hammer sex-vampire movie seems largely to have been promoted by the independent producer Harry Fine, a former television casting director of series like *William Tell*, before he graduated to producing slick exploitation-orientated features with director Peter Collinson (*The Penthouse*, *Up the Junction*). This was around the time that the old Hammer hierarchy was breaking up, and several independent producers moved in to do work for the company. Fine had decided that the vampire story which most deserved updating for the seventies was Le Fanu's *Carmilla*.

In fact *Carmilla* had been adapted twice for the screen since 1960, when Vadim used the story for his own *Et Mourir de Plaisir* (*Blood and Roses*). In some ways this was the original sex-vampire movie, though even Vadim could not at this time approach the novel's overt physicality. He had to content himself with a series of suggestive images and one lingering shot of the rain washing the women's faces as they kiss. Vadim did however make some intriguing alterations in Le Fanu's narrative, updating it to a story of possession in an Italian baronial setting and actually using a first person narration from Carmilla's point of view. He also added a strong Surrealist undertone, via some black-and-white dream footage of waiting rooms and hospital surgeries, which echo the

The further adventures of Carmilla Karnstein, now played by Yutte Stensgaard in *Lust for a Vampire*. Script-writer Jimmy Sangster places her ingeniously in a girls' finishing school, where she captivates teachers and pupils alike.

analytical reading of *Dracula* as a memory of a child's trauma at the hands of surgeons and hospitals.

The other *Carmilla* adaptation, *Terror in the Crypt* (1963) had been a stodgy and confused Italian rehash of the theme. Since neither of these films had had a great deal of impact on international audiences, Harry Fine and his partner Michael Style felt the time was right for Hammer to mount an explicit reworking of *Carmilla* which would include all the lesbian passion which Le Fanu had woven into his original. Unfortunately, perhaps, they cast Ingrid Pitt in the lead, an actress who in no way resembled Le Fanu's creation of a teenage girl 'slender, and wonderfully graceful. Except

that her movements were languid — *very* languid . . . her features were small and beautifully formed, her eyes large, dark and lustrous.'

But Pitt, a Polish émigrée who had been working in Italian and Spanish movies, was able to add a strident erotic quality to the part that suited it quite well, and the rest of the casting was better: Pippa Steele and Madeleine Smith both had the right kind of naive girlish-ness to be Carmilla's adolescent victims, while Peter Cushing, Douglas Wilmer and Jon Finch provided vampire-hunting support.

Solidly directed by Roy Baker, *The Vampire Lovers* begins with a sequence of the kind of intense dream-like beauty which was to crop

up from time to time in the two sequels that followed: a young man watches the shrouded figure of a vampire floating mistily towards him. Suddenly to his amazement, it reveals itself as a shimmeringly beautiful young girl (a nice introduction to Hammer's alteration of the vampire's image) and as he stands transfixed, her breast touches his crucifix and he destroys her.

This is one of the film's few sequences that is pure invention. The rest of it follows *Carmilla* extremely carefully, even down to the conversation about death when the vampire seems to be scared of the possibility of mortality ('I hate funerals'). The early furtive courtship of the two girls is handled by Baker with a minimum

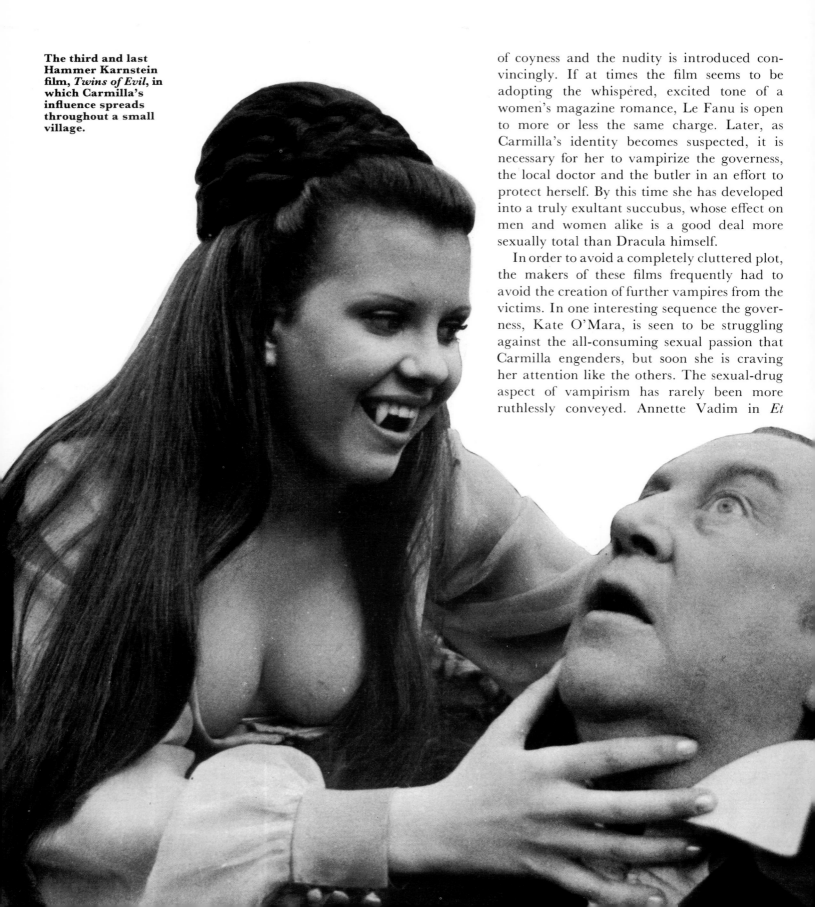

The third and last Hammer Karnstein film, *Twins of Evil*, in which Carmilla's influence spreads throughout a small village.

of coyness and the nudity is introduced convincingly. If at times the film seems to be adopting the whispered, excited tone of a women's magazine romance, Le Fanu is open to more or less the same charge. Later, as Carmilla's identity becomes suspected, it is necessary for her to vampirize the governess, the local doctor and the butler in an effort to protect herself. By this time she has developed into a truly exultant succubus, whose effect on men and women alike is a good deal more sexually total than Dracula himself.

In order to avoid a completely cluttered plot, the makers of these films frequently had to avoid the creation of further vampires from the victims. In one interesting sequence the governess, Kate O'Mara, is seen to be struggling against the all-consuming sexual passion that Carmilla engenders, but soon she is craving her attention like the others. The sexual-drug aspect of vampirism has rarely been more ruthlessly conveyed. Annette Vadim in *Et*

Mourir de Plaisir seems an enormously muted incarnation of Carmilla beside it.

Lust for a Vampire directed by Jimmy Sangster which followed hard on the heels of the success of *The Vampire Lovers* at the box office, took the image of the omnipotent female sex goddess to even greater lengths. Apart from the dreadful song which the makers saw fit to dub over one amorous encounter ('Strange love,' drools the vocal) and some script blunders, it is one of the most enjoyable sex-vampire films Hammer made.

Sangster, who had returned to Hammer for a brief period before leaving England for America, was easily able to utilize the new developments as a vehicle for the black humour that had been a continuing aspect of his approach to horror since his first *Curse of Frankenstein* script. Although *Lust for a Vampire* was written (at times rather ploddingly) by the writer of *The Vampire Lovers*, Tudor Gates, Sangster exploited to the full an overtly ludicrous plot about a nineteenth-century girls' finishing school which turns up near Karnstein castle like some heaven-sent butcher's shop. Carmilla naturally enrolls as a pupil and runs amok among girls and staff, as the film uses all the visual devices at the director's disposal to convey an aura of potent cloying sensuality. The resulting movie is full of furtive adolescent vampirizing behind locked doors, whispered assignations by moonlit lakes and the petty sexual intrigues of the classroom and the dormitory. In one audacious tracking shot, Sangster even allows his camera to become Mircalla, stalking her victim.

Stylistically Sangster's direction is on the right side of parody, but he is thwarted by the script's more idiotic interpolations like the sub-Dracula appearance of Mike Raven as Count Karnstein, and the plot's disintegration into a static mystery story as the headmistress of the school covers up a succession of bodies. Le Fanu himself has been put into the action as English writer Richard Lestrange, who falls in love with Mircalla and in return is accorded

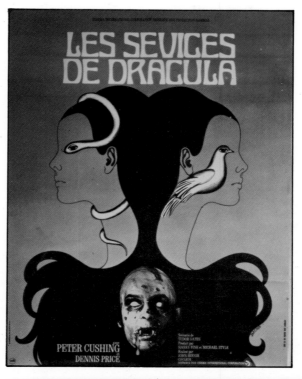

A French poster for *Twins of Evil.*

Black magic ceremony in the Karnstein castle in *Twins of Evil.*

Madeleine Collinson, perhaps the most relentless of all Hammer's sex-vampires, engages in the highly ambiguous infantile vampirism of *Twins of Evil*.

One of the victims of the Puritans in *Twins of Evil*.

Baron Karnstein (Damien Thomas) has been transformed into a vampire by his ancestress Carmilla.

the vampiric affection that was described with an ingenious evasiveness in the original text as 'an engrossing vehemence resembling the passion of love'. But the sheer extent of the sexual devastation caused by Mircalla in *Lust for a Vampire* makes her seem not so much an enchanting bisexual *femme fatale* as a creature of science fiction, a highly tuned and monstrous libido machine. Yutte Stensgaard's impassive doll-like features only accentuate the effect.

Later that year Hammer did their own Countess Bathory story, *Countess Dracula*, attempting a more Gothic period reconstruction of the myth. Ingrid Pitt played the title role, alternating between aged crone and seductress depending on how recently she had bathed in virgin's blood. It was a crudely 'magical' reading of the legend, though the murders were carried out with surprising relish, notably a protracted encounter with a prostitute, which still seems lucky to have passed untouched by the censor. The notable thing about *Countess Dracula* was that it continued director Peter Sasdy's preoccupation with the vampiric destruction of the family from *Taste the Blood of Dracula*, chronicling the symbolic disintegration of the Bathory line as she consumes her daughter's personality and finally the girl's body for the blood she needs. The cruel anti-maternal theme was amplified by several mocking references to breasts and motherhood, and by the mother's ambivalent maternal/sexual relations with her lover.

Twins of Evil in 1971 was yet another movie very loosely based on Le Fanu, though this time the figure of the engulfing female vampire is transmuted into a pair of sultry twins (Madeleine and Mary Collinson). The stodgy Tudor Gates script, involving a battle between puritans and vampires, became even more rambling than before, so that the film presented almost exactly the same combination of ingredients in a less attractive package. But the two demented and irredeemably evil girl vampires at the plot's centre are noticeable for presenting the 'libido machine' at its most

extreme. There is one shot in which a lethal crucifix virtually comes into contact with the vampire's exposed pubic hair which, in its vicious juxtaposition of sexual energy and religious discipline, matches anything that Rollin, for all his overt Surrealism, has yet achieved.

The Vampire Circus, one of Hammer's last attempts at the field, tried to adapt the sex-vampire into a denser and more complex structure. A medieval village, suffering from the curse of the staked vampire Count Mitterhouse, is visited by plague and then a mysterious travelling circus. The show turns out to be a front for the vampires, and gradually it comes to represent all the qualities of sensual wonder and suppressed erotic excitement which the villagers have blocked. There are some evocative sequences when, for example, the circus acrobats are transformed into bats before the onlookers' eyes, and a panther turns into a man. Unfortunately the plot contains as many characters as a Gothic novel, but it succeeds in weaving a delicate aura of mystery around the circus, and theoretically it should have worked very well.

The film-maker's problem seems to have arisen precisely because the sexually explicit elements were now *de rigueur*, and had to be included. As a (somewhat simplified) story in the old Hammer manner, *The Vampire Circus* could have been successful. But despite its better moments, it finally seems boring and meretricious. The film's inherent contradictions are clearly expressed when Count Mitterhouse momentarily turns his attention away from the victim's neck to a full sexual embrace with a muttered, 'One lust feeds the other.' It is a line that will almost invariably get an unsympathetic laugh from audiences. And it deserves some kind of immortality, because it so clearly demonstrates the film-maker's impasse when confronted with the commercial necessity of including material which is utterly wrong for his film.

The sex-vampire had automatically dispersed the established cinematic tradition of the vampire, with the result that many lesser genre film-makers were in some confusion.

THE NEW AMERICAN VAMPIRE

'The grim and grisly ranks of the Undead'

The American cinema of the 1960s witnessed an intriguing transformation of the vampire into the ghoul, vividly demonstrated by the followers of Count Yorga in *The Return of Count Yorga*.

Roger Corman's films have been the inspiration of countless spin-offs. *Little Shop of Horrors,* his film about a vampire plant, starred Mel Welles, who went on to direct his own vampire film on the same theme, *Island of the Doomed*.

IN ANY DISCUSSION of American exploitation pictures during the 1950s and 1960s one name is almost certain to crop up. Roger Corman was one of the few American film-makers who actively resisted the tendency of the major Hollywood studios to concede British dominance in the horror field. His most successful weapon was the continuing popularity of Edgar Allan Poe as a horror writer, and Corman built Poe's world into a native American Gothic subject with its own marketability. Poe of course had never tackled the vampire theme, because he died in 1849 before it became a staple of Gothic literature, but Corman approached it on a few occasions in his non-Poe films and his tough yet intelligent approach to pulp movie-making had a direct effect on the way the vampire film now developed in America.

Roger Corman was a native of Los Angeles who graduated from Beverley Hills High School in the early 1940s and then took a degree in engineering. His career as an engineer was interrupted by three years in the navy, and he subsequently worked as a messenger and script editor for Twentieth-Century Fox, before leaving for a post-graduate literary course at Oxford University in England.

When he returned to Hollywood as a literary agent, this varied intellectual background made him a little unusual in the parochial world of post-war Hollywood. And his enormous business shrewdness, together with a seemingly boundless energy, soon enabled him to put together a cheapie crime movie called *Highway Dragnet* with Richard Conte and Joan Bennett. After producing a couple of similar efforts, Corman realized that he could direct as efficiently and economically as anyone else and he made his first film as producer/director in 1955: *Five Guns West*. But he was increasingly drawn to horror and science-fiction themes because of their commercial viability and by 1956 he put together one of the more interesting amalgamations of science fiction and vampirism called *Not of This Earth*.

The idea of a blood parasite from outer space had been promulgated in several American films from *The Thing* onwards, but Corman was the first to give the vampire a more human delineation. A bulky male figure wearing sinister thick-lensed sunglasses, he has the air of a ruthless and misanthropic businessman rather than an alien. After he has terrorized a teenage girl (in a hilarious 'night' sequence, complete with hooting owl, which was evidently filmed in broad daylight), he obtains an interview with a doctor and then removes his sunglasses to reveal blank white eyes behind the lenses. The use of contact lenses was later to become a rather corny feature of the Hammer Dracula, but here it worked well, especially in the 'normal' mid-American setting. Endowed like so many screen vampires with an aggressive power of hypnosis, the alien calling himself Paul Johnson (Paul Birch) reveals that the inhabitants of his planet are suffering from a blood deficiency and intend to utilize the earth as a giant blood bank, 'pasturing' its inhabitants.

On the doctor's instructions a special nurse is assigned to Johnson's home to give him blood, but the murders continue as he desperately teleports blood to his dying planet. Finally he is joined by another alien who is destroyed by the blood of a rabid dog, and after a chase Johnson's car topples over a cliff. But as the hero piously stands over his grave marked 'Here lies a man not of this earth', a familiar bulky and bespectacled figure lumbers across the cemetery towards him.

There are many clumsy moments in *Not of This Earth*, but given the paucity of Corman's resources it remains relatively sophisticated of its kind, with one or two relevant ideas. The figure of the vampire himself is well conceived, accentuating the normal into the grotesque with a bare minimum of special effects. The use of medical imagery also indicated one of the possibilities open to the modern vampire film, which would occasionally be developed.

Not of This Earth owed a great deal to its writer, Charles B. Griffith, a devotee of fantasy literature, who had himself published science-fiction and horror stories. In 1960 he collabora-

**The giant flesh-eating
plant in Roger
Corman's comedy
vampire film, *Little
Shop of Horrors*.**

ted with Corman on another variation on the vampire theme in *Little Shop of Horrors*, a film which has become a legend because it was completed during the course of a long weekend ('We were going to play tennis but it was raining,' is Corman's celebrated account of the reason for its production). This time the bloodsucker is a ludicrous species of plant, which developed a taste for blood when its creator Seymour Mushnick (Jonathan Haze) accidentally sprinkled it with blood from a cut finger. From then on he is forced to satisfy its demands for human flesh by feeding it the odd corpse, until its appetite becomes insatiable. Finally, just at the moment when Seymour is presented with a horticultural trophy, all the plant's buds open to reveal the reflected faces of its victims. At the end of his tether, Seymour feeds himself to the plant, -carrying a knife.

This was virtually the first horror movie Corman made which was specifically tailored as a comedy and he almost succeeds in bringing it off. The plant itself was the *reductio ad absurdum* of the vampiric appetite, whining 'Feed me!' Its leaves bulge and quiver as it swallows gangsters whole, while regurgitating their guns. There were also admirable contributions from Corman's regular stock company including a tiny appearance from Jack Nicholson as an ardent masochist. If the film is finally deflated by the repetition that is an inevitable result of such a crippling budget, it still comes nearer than most of its successors to making vampires into a good comedy subject.

Apart from the recent Andy Warhol *Dracula* discussed later, there are two other main cinematic contenders in this limited field. They are Polanski's *Dance of the Vampires*, and *The Cloak* episode from Amicus's *House That Dripped Blood*, the latter written by the noted American fantasy writer Robert Bloch. *The Cloak* is a potentially amusing sketch, concocted for Christopher Lee, about a star of *Dracula* movies whose screen persona is so greatly admired by the undead that they lure him into their

clutches with the help of a magical cloak. The idea of getting Lee to play himself might very well have come off, but he finally decided against the part and in a moment of folly the producers abandoned the whole original conception and cast a comedy actor (Jon Pertwee) instead of a horror actor to play it. This effectively ruined the whole conception and farce was substituted for irony.

Dance of the Vampires is more formidable because it was made in England by one of the most talented of all horror movie-makers, Roman Polanski, as a conscious pastiche of the Hammer vampire movie (specifically *Kiss of the Vampire* and *Brides of Dracula*). The production had a high budget, some good sets and locations plus a talented production crew, yet it turned out to be less funny than *Little Shop of Horrors* and was a box-office disaster. In America the distributors even tried a desperate salvage operation, re-dubbing and re-editing, but this only made matters worse.

The failure of Polanski's film, in which the eccentric vampire hunter Professor Abronsius (Jack MacGowran) and his witless assistant (Polanski himself) are on the trail of Count Von Krolock (played by Ferdy Mayne), suggests what had always been suspected: that the Gothic vampire genre exists on a knife-edge between audience involvement on the one hand, and cynical boredom on the other, that the merest slip is likely to bring the whole thing down. Polanski did not just slip, he flung himself over. Not content with casting comedy actors in most of the key parts, the script keeps harping on its own lack of seriousness with a nudging insistence that the plot's framework simply cannot withstand. The result is long periods of boredom when the action fails to engage on any level. *Little Shop of Horrors*, on the other hand, for all its many faults and tedious passages, manages to avoid this pitfall principally because it is not a traditional vampire plot, and is not subject to the same constraints. Corman's ability with comedy was later proven by *The Raven* which is perhaps the closest that anyone has got to a successful Gothic farce in the movies other than Warhol, but it kept well away from vampires.

Intriguingly, one of the actors in *Little Shop of Horrors*, Mel Welles, went on to readapt its plot into a more conventional horror movie, *Island of the Doomed* (British title: *Bloodsuckers*), an undistinguished Spanish/German co-production of 1966 about a man-eating tree. Corman himself became increasingly involved with the Poe series and never returned to the vampire as a subject, but several of his protégés did. In fact, he was to be instrumental in the career of the first woman to direct vampire movies: Stephanie Rothman.

In the meantime, in the early sixties, a few desultory American vampire films had explored unprofitable seams like the vampire western. *Curse of the Undead* (Edward Dein) had inaugurated this trend in 1959, with a black-clad

John Carradine as the ludicrous Dracula figure in Al Adamson's *The Blood of Dracula's Castle.*

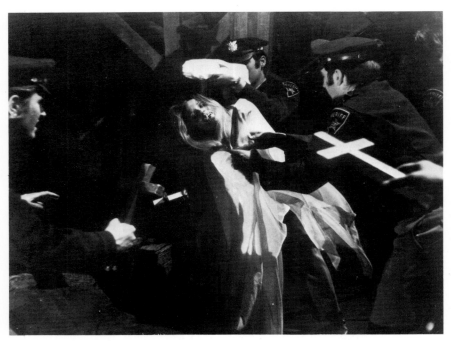

The vampire-hunting patrolmen in Dan Curtis's *House of Dark Shadows*, a film version of his successful American television series *Dark Shadows*.

gunslinger who sleeps in a coffin and is finally laid to rest by a cross etched in a bullet. *Billy the Kid vs. Dracula* (William Beaudine, 1966) actually features John Carradine as a Dracula-figure whose activities come near to starting an Indian uprising before he is exorcised. In contrast, the undistinguished output of Al Adamson worked more on the basis that the word 'blood' was a Drive-In certainty, including *The Blood of Dracula's Castle, Blood of Frankenstein* (sometimes known as *Frankenstein vs. Dracula*) and *Horror of the Blood Monsters* in quick succession, at the end of the sixties. All three are so depleted in conception and realization that they rank even lower than the later Universal pictures, the last one being padded out with footage from two anonymous Philippine productions.

Some critics have been driven to describe basically incompetent manifestations of the horror movie like Adamson's work as 'horror comics', but the description is grossly unfair to the comics. EC, the largest producers who were driven out of the field by censorship in 1954, had in their five-year run provided enough plots and visual ideas to fuel a whole rebirth of the horror movie in America. In fact, if the pulp film-makers of the fifties and sixties had only emulated their style, they would

have produced far better films. But they lacked the talent to do this, and could not steal the stories which were subject to a jealously guarded copyright by their publisher William Gaines.

Very occasionally the vigorously graphic style of EC creeps into the American horror movie (Philip Gilbert's *Blood and Lace* is a rare example). Gaines did not intend to surrender the rights until he was sure they would be handled with a proper respect for the original. In the end, he did allow the British company Amicus to re-adapt the comics as episode horror movies and amongst the stories Milton Subotsky selected was Joe Orlando's classic vampire tale *Midnight Mess*.

This episode is about a man visiting his sister in an old town, where he is constantly regaled by warnings about vampires. He cannot sleep during the night and goes out for a walk, during which he comes across a busy, crowded restaurant. Entering it, he is struck by the strangeness of the waiters and customers. The food tastes salty. Then in the mirror he sees that he is the only diner. The restaurant is run by the undead, and his sister turns out to be one of them: 'In the OLD DAYS,' she now tells him with suitable comic books emphasis, 'HUMANS HUNTED THEIR OWN FOOD . . . PREPARED it themselves! VAMPIRES TOO in the legends, hunted THEIR OWN VICTIMS! But now, WE, just like MODERN MAN, leave the HUNTING to the PROFESSIONALS! We leave the PREPARING to the professionals, TOO . . .'. Whereupon the hero is strung up and a tap is inserted into his jugular as the vampires have a barbecue party ('Nothin' like the REAL STUFF!' says one of them jubilantly filling his glass).

As a horror story, *Midnight Mess* combines the right ingredients of accumulating mystery with a shocking yet witty climax. The ending is both horrible and humorous, so grotesque that it is impossible to take it seriously and yet so glibly plausible and appalling that its impact remains unaffected by self-

La Fiancée du Vampire

METRO-GOLDWYN-MAYER présente UNE PRODUCTION DAN CURTIS   LA FIANCÉE DU VAMPIRE avec JONATHAN FRID et GRAYSON HALL

et JOAN BENNETT dans le rôle d'Elizabeth Collins Stoddard avec KATHRYN LEIGH SCOTT · ROGER DAVIS · NANCY BARRETT · JOHN KARLEN · LOUIS EDMONDS · DONALD BRISCOE
Scénario de SAM HALL et GORDON RUSSELL · Produit et mis en scène par DAN CURTIS · METROCOLOR
Interdit aux moins de 13 ans

A French poster for Dan Curtis's *House of Dark Shadows*.

Overleaf: **Amicus's adaptations of the notorious but intensely imaginative EC horror comics of the fifties rarely conveyed the style of the original. Only the last shot of the vampire story, *Midnight Mess*, in the episode film *Vault of Horror* really attempts to reproduce the crudely effective graphic style of artist Joe Orlando. Illustration © 1977 by William M. Gaines.**

American International's Yorga series, inaugurated by *Count Yorga Vampire*, concentrated as much on the grisly activities of Yorga's brides as on the vampire himself.

parody. Nominally it should have been ideal for the cinema, but in the 1973 production, *Vault of Horror*, it suffered from the patchy quality that afflicts almost all of the Amicus episode horror movies.

Instead of sticking to the original plot Milton Subotsky invented a completely new beginning about a man murdering his sister. This immediately alters the pace of the whole thing, substituting a mechanistic, fugitive feeling for the original's gradual intrusion of the normal into the abnormal, and smashing the audience's identification with the main character. It also spoils the surprise of the sister's transformation: a corpse is a far more threatening possibility in a horror movie than a nice relative, so her reappearance as a vengeful vampire comes as no surprise at all and the ending is merely a gruesome revenge rather than a total dislocation of narrative. Visually too, Roy Ward Baker makes little attempt to duplicate the quality of Orlando's frame composition, except in the last shot. Although Amicus have done a couple of fair EC stories (*Reflections of Death* in *Tales From the Crypt* is probably the best screen evocation of the EC style), William Gaines still has to wait for a really impressive screen recreation of his work.

There were a few other pulp film vampires in the sixties that vaguely hinted at the EC tone in their choice of theme if in nothing else. David Durston's *I Drink Your Blood* features a boy infecting a gang of murderous hippies with rabies by putting dog's blood into meat pies and the film ends with a crazed confrontation between the maddened hippies and construction workers. Much more interesting was Richard Matheson's made-for-TV feature *The Night Stalker* in which the reporter-hero tracks and kills a vampire killer of superhuman strength in contemporary Las Vegas.

The use of a taut documentary-style police format was a deft Matheson contribution to the Gothic cinema, and the producer of *The Night Stalker*, Dan Curtis, has utilized the idea numerous times since in features like *The Norliss*

The imagery of the vampire cinema had become more intensely sadistic by the late sixties, as in this scene from *Count Yorga Vampire*.

Tapes. The theme of many of these movies is the hero's potentially posthumous account of his struggle with the supernatural relayed by manuscript or tape as a last defiant rebuke to the authorities who disbelieved him. But a somewhat less sceptical police force had been available to the heroes of Dan Curtis's *House of Dark Shadows* (a spin-off from his American television series *Dark Shadows*), which is most notable for its squads of patrolmen brandishing crucifixes.

Despite Curtis's attempts to build Kolckack from *The Night Stalker* and Barnabas from *Dark Shadows* into new genre figures, only two screen vampires have really achieved some kind of international recognition since the sixties, and so far neither of them has survived more than two films.

Count Yorga, probably the more interesting of the pair, was originally conceived as a character in a routine softcore porno movie by producer George Macready. But his friend, the actor Robert Quarry, who was a horror-movie fan read the script and persuaded him to try and make the film into a proper horror story with Quarry in the lead. They were lucky too to join forces with an imaginative film-maker called Robert Kelljan who wrote the film and worked small wonders with the minute budget. Quarry himself quotes the figure as $20,000 which, if true, must rank as some kind of record for a successful genre movie. Even *Night of the Living Dead*, the seminal horror film of the late sixties (discussed later in this chapter) cost $125,000 to shoot in black and white under exceptionally primitive conditions. If *Yorga* was even as cheap to make as Quarry claims, it is not surprising that the film was so profitable that AIP was prepared to finance a much more lavish sequel the following year. *The Return of Count Yorga* improved on the original conception in almost every respect, but there the series has rested.

If Yorga represents the most interesting attempt to bring Count Dracula to a modern urban setting, it is because his creators have at least made an effort to solve some of the problems involved. The Count himself is in physical appearance a rather stale recreation of the Latin vampire, with hair thinning at the temples and an oily formality (as opposed to the original's civilized charm). But the characters in the film voice the audience's own scepticism towards him, commenting directly on the anachronism of his appearance, and his resemblance to a vampire. Having thus flirted with our incredulity, Kelljan juxtaposes these lighter moments with a series of blood attacks that are extremely violent – far more so than the vampirism of the Hammer movies. Although Yorga does utilize hypnotic attraction on potential recruits (even on one occasion in front of a girl's unsuspecting boyfriend) his bloodsucking is generally prefixed by nothing gentler than a clawing, snarling sprint towards the victim. His attentions are far more immediately devastating than Dracula's, but he is also able to hold his own in civilized society.

In the first film, Kelljan's approach to this dichotomy is crude but by the second it had been refined into a potent weapon. Much of *Count Yorga Vampire* is in any case concerned

The resurrection sequence in Hammer's *Plague of the Zombies* had a strong influence on several horror films, especially *The Return of Count Yorga*.

with the mechanical aspect of setting up the plot. Yorga's coffin is unloaded in Los Angeles harbour, he conducts a séance with some teenagers and brings one of the girls under his hypnotic control. The film picks up with an eerie night at Yorga's mansion, after which one of the girls is found inexplicably devouring a cat in her apartment.

Now the script deliberately pauses as the characters try to come to terms with the idea of vampirism and desperately ponder the appropriate methods of disposal ('Vampires, you've got to be kidding', etc.). It picks up again with the climax in Yorga's mansion as the heroes confront a mass attack of female vampires in their efforts to rescue a missing girl. When the hero finally emerges unscathed after all the other vampires are staked, the rescued heroine turns on him, revealing her fangs. This climax caused a big audience reaction when the film appeared, as it was almost the first serious genre vampire movie to break the convention of the happy ending.

But *The Return of Count Yorga* was a huge improvement on its predecessor. Robert Kelljan had evidently studied the uneasy, paranoid tone of *Night of the Living Dead* and he incorporated as much of it as he could into the film, which benefits from locations near San Francisco. A little orphan boy is playing innocently in a graveyard near Yorga's castle and suddenly living corpses begin to churn their way up from the soil and advance towards him in a nightmarish, crumbling mass. Then Yorga appears, and Kelljan shock-cuts to a folksy, fund-raising orphanage party, the 'normality' of which appears if anything more bizarre than what we have already seen, as the guests parade their fancy dress. Count Yorga's appearance at the party is completely congruous, because most of the men have turned up as half-hearted Draculas, and he is immediately attracted to Cynthia Nelson (Mariette Hartley), the assistant of the orphanage's principal. The party breaks up when a guest is wounded by an unknown attacker, and later that night Yorga

sends his voracious tribe of vampires to massacre Cynthia's family.

The assault is a crazed mindless orgy of destruction; Yorga's vampires are not elegant sensual females but decrepit animal-like hags who shuffle clumsily towards their victims with dreadful perseverance. Cynthia becomes a prisoner in Yorga's castle and Yorga has hypnotized her into forgetting what she has seen, but her fiancé David (Roger Perry) becomes suspicious. After several more murders, the police finally agree to explore Yorga's castle. In the ensuing battle David survives to destroy Yorga, and Cynthia kisses him in relief, only to find that he is now a vampire.

The Return of Count Yorga is vigorously directed, and Kelljan makes numerous sly observations in it, frequently pointing up the absurdist aspect of middle-American society. He seems especially interested in its uneasy preoccupation with violent fantasy, a theme which is first introduced at the party and returns when even Yorga himself is seen enjoying some bloodsucking on television.

The implication seems to be that America gets the vampires it deserves and that, in the context of the country's homicide figures, a genocidal Count from Transylvania is hardly impossible, or even remarkable. Unfortunately Yorga's characterization occasionally gets in the way of the painstakingly elaborated atmosphere, as when he is allowed to assume a camp romantic posture and speak lines like, 'The most fragile emotion ever known has entered my breast.' But counterpointing this whimsical aspect is the unceasing line of blood-spattered, hag-like brides who lack any of the redeeming erotic grace of earlier movie vampires. Bob Kelljan might just have been able to give the Dracula-character a new lease of urban life if the Yorga cycle had not been so abruptly terminated.

There never seemed to be much hope of this with the other genre vampire of the seventies. If Yorga was a happy and profitable accident, *Blacula* was the product of pure financial

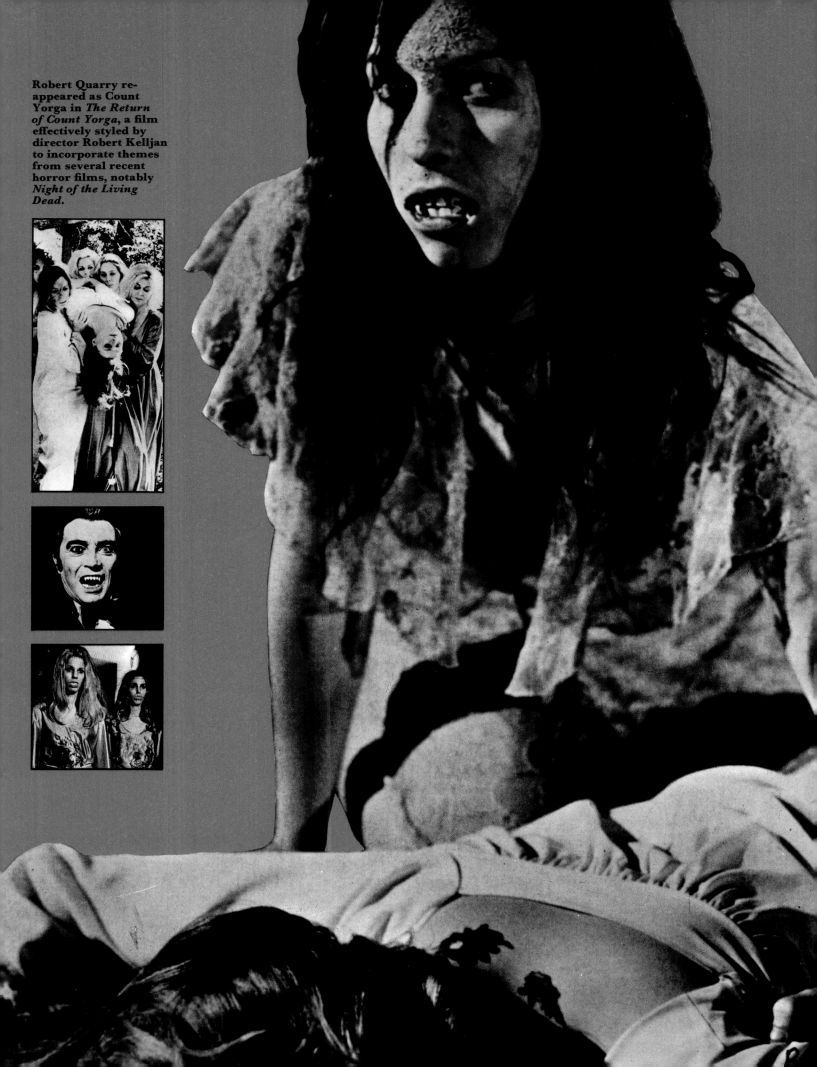

Robert Quarry re-appeared as Count Yorga in *The Return of Count Yorga*, a film effectively styled by director Robert Kelljan to incorporate themes from several recent horror films, notably *Night of the Living Dead*.

Prior to *The Velvet Vampire* Stephanie Rothman made *Student Nurses*, an exploitation movie, for Roger Corman.

expediency. By 1972, in the wake of black heroes like Shaft, Hollywood had finally become aware of the vast profits that could be made out of black audiences. On this basis, it decided that most of the major movies of the past could be given a black orientation and remade as cheaply and mechanically as possible. Of course, theoretically, the idea of a black 'Dracula' could have been exciting. Just as Stoker's original drew much of his power from the sexual guilt of Victorian England, so a black Dracula let loose in contemporary America might have effectively provided a focus for the guilt and neurosis of the dominant white culture.

With uncharacteristic timidity, however, American International Pictures never once allowed this kind of suggestion to enter their film, except perhaps in its feeble prologue where a spokesman for the black nations fleetingly appears at Count Dracula's castle, hoping the Count will help him put an end to the slave trade. Dracula responds in the usual manner, with the result that the freedom fighter becomes the vampire Blacula and is imprisoned in a coffin until two gay antique dealers ship his body back to Los Angeles. Blacula claims the antique merchants as his first victims and the rest of the tiresome script is concerned with the worst of all horror clichés, that is, the monster's quest for a reincarnation of his lost love. He finds her in a girl called Tina, but after her friend's suspicions are aroused, the police close in on Blacula's lair in an electrical factory and Tina is staked while the lovelorn Blacula rushes out to disintegrate in the sunlight.

Wᴵᴸᴸᴵᴬᴹ Marshall plays Blacula in the tradition of black nobility associated with Othello, but the plot and direction give him almost nothing of any interest to do and the rest of the characters are routine comic caricatures. *Scream Blacula Scream* (1973) is an improvement, being directed by Robert Kelljan of the Yorga series, although the plot is in the pseudo-tragic tradition of *House of Dracula*.

Once again, the vampire seeks a cure for his condition, this time through the black magic cult of voodoo and he falls in love with the voodoo priestess (played by Pam Grier). But Kelljan manages to make this potentially sentimental strain a little more palatable by juxtaposing it with the vampire's obvious loathing for modern society, especially in his contemptuous killing of two street-pimps which oddly prefigures the climax of Scorsese's *Taxi Driver*.

Aᴹᴼᴿᴱ promising diversification for the vampire than *Blacula* has emerged from the work of Stephanie Rothman, one of the few women working in commercial features and the first woman ever to make a vampire movie. She studied in the graduate course in cinema at the University of Southern California and followed it with a fellowship from the Director's Guild of America, during which she worked for some time as an assistant to Roger Corman. Corman's help and sponsorship, which has played such a major part in the American genre movie scene, enabled her to direct a series of pictures.

The first was *Blood Bath*, alternatively titled *Track of the Vampire*, in 1966. Co-directed and co-written with Jack Hill, this was an odd amalgamation of the old *House of Wax*-type plot with the undead: an artist, who is the reincarnation of a vampire, drinks his models' blood and then uses their corpses as the basis of his work. After this first tentative stab at the theme, she made *It's a Bikini World* in 1967 and three years later the intriguing *Student Nurses* for Corman.

Then in 1971, Rothman attempted a far more ambitious vampire picture, *The Velvet Vampire*, which occasionally came near to being a feminist answer to the Yorga movies. Celeste Yarnall plays a lesbian-inclined vampire with a liking for velvet who, in a deft tribute to the creator of the lesbian undead, is named Diane Le Fanu. She meets a young couple at an art exhibition in the 'Stoker' gallery and lures them back to her desert home. There they

gradually grasp her real nature and the movie ends with a spectacular chase through Los Angeles.

Stephanie Rothman manages the same overall intelligence and style which Kelljan had brought to the Yorga movies, utilizing the hippie milieu of southern California as a conveniently fantasy-orientated setting. There is also the same pre-*Taxi Driver* quality, notable in *Scream Blacula Scream*, this time given a feminist twist when Diane turns her attentions on a mugger/rapist. Of course, by the early seventies California already had the connotations of mass murder and hypnotic mind-control that had been generated by the Manson murders. Robert Quarry and director Ray Danton made the explicit connection between Manson and vampire in an opportunistic little movie

called *The Deathmaster* about a vampire who is washed ashore in California.

But the seventies also saw two more official American reappearances of Count Dracula, although both of them were shot in Europe. Paul Morrissey's *Blood for Dracula*, produced under the seal of Andy Warhol, is a gory humorous sexploitation comedy which doesn't work nearly as well as the Frankenstein adaptation which had preceded it. Udo Kier plays the demented and wheelchair-ridden Count who is forced to leave Transylvania in search of more 'wurrgin's blaad'. With his impertinent assistant, he takes to his regal motor car and travels to Roman Catholic Italy where he encounters an incomprehensible nobleman (Vittorio De Sica) and four daughters. Unfortunately most of the children have been

William Marshall as the militant black vampire in *Blacula*, a film conceived and shot to a strict formula.

compromised by gardener Joe Dallesandro, and consequently whenever the Count manages to get his hands on them he is sent spluttering blood and vomit to the nearest toilet. Finally, as he pursues the only virgin daughter through the castle, she is rescued by Dallesandro who pushes her against the wall explaining, 'It's the only way to save you.' The death-scene has the miserable Count being chased by Dallesandro with an axe, until every limb has been systematically chopped and there is nothing left to stake.

Udo Kier has an immaculate seriousness that could have made him the funniest comic Dracula yet (he is certainly the funniest Baron Frankenstein). He is able to suggest impotent outrage and self-pity by every distorted syllable and expression, without ever letting the façade of conviction crack. Theoretically he presented the perfect inversion of Dracula, a man who grossly over-values his effect on others. But Morrissey's script very quickly dissolves into a mechanical repetition of sex and gore, with only a few early jokes like the Count's almost babyish insistence on his need for food as a reminder of what it might have been.

Dan Curtis's orthodox adaptation of Bram Stoker was made in 1974 in Britain for American television with, of all people, Jack Palance trying his hand at the role. Although adapted by Richard Matheson, who tried to remain faithful to the original, the results were immensely disappointing. For some reason Matheson took it upon himself to give the Count a cod-Freudian motive for his activities, so that we are continually treated to dewy-eyed flashbacks of his lost love, punctuated by a mawkish tinkling score. Moreover Palance, with his thuggish good looks, is painfully unsuited to the role of a decadent aristocrat and even, in the more menacing moments, his cod-Lugosi performance places him at two removes from the original. Van Helsing becomes a solid Englishman rather than a Quixotic rational/mystical foreigner, while vampirism itself has been relegated almost to the level of a

minor character obsession. These major blunders make the production's occasional concern with detail (like the first proper utilization of Whitby in a Dracula film) all the more frustrating. The extraordinary thing about both Dan Curtis's and Jess Franco's recent attempts to reproduce Bram Stoker is that in their (by no means consistent) attention to minutiae, they both overlook the fact that Stoker's novel is constructed as a thriller.

By far the most influential and innovatory recent American vampire movie is usually characterized as a film about ghouls or zombies. But the protagonists of George Romero's *Night of the Living Dead* accurately fulfill both of the stipulations laid down by Ernest Jones in his definition of vampires in *On the Nightmare*: '. . . the two essential characteristics of a true vampire are thus his origins in a dead person and his habit of sucking blood.' In fact the film presented what is probably the only truly modernist reading of the vampire myth, and for this reason its theme and technique have been subject to constant imitation. Almost all of the new American vampires from Yorga to Blacula have lifted ideas from *Night of the Living Dead* without being able to duplicate its sophistication.

Night of the Living Dead was made by a tiny production company in Pittsburgh on an erratic production schedule that lasted nine months from 1967 to 1968. Most of the cast were amateurs, apart from the two leads, and Romero shot it in monochrome for budgetary reasons, using natural light for the daytime exteriors. This technique gave some of the film, particularly the opening, a grainy, sombre quality, reminiscent of Dreyer's *Vampyr* or Gerard Gibbs's photography for Hammer's science fiction of the 1950s. The inspiration for the story (written by Romero and screenwriter John Russo) seems to be Richard Matheson's *I Am Legend*. The film is closer to the authentic spirit of Matheson's modern vampire novel than any of the official screen adaptations. But its plot is filtered through the

**A French poster for
Mario Bava's** *Mask of
the Demon.*

ruptured America of the 1960s, a society tormented by rising crime at home and a divisive war overseas.

Night of the Living Dead begins with the grown-up brother and sister of an ordinary middle-American family driving out to the lonely Pennsylvanian graveyard where their father is buried. It is a dreary Sunday night in autumn and the clocks have just been changed; the landscape is bleak and deserted. They arrive at the graveside with Johnny grumbling about the futility of the trip: the dead are dead. His irritation turns to frivolity and he starts to tease his sister Barbara, who is slightly uneasy in the gathering dusk.

Far away in the distance, through the trees, a solitary man can be seen walking towards them. There is something slightly clumsy about his stride, but he is just a single man, hardly a threat or even a curiosity. As he approaches Johnny idly incorporates him into his teasing: 'They're coming for you,' he moans. Barbara is caught in the classic impasse (so rarely portrayed in horror films) of fear and embarrassment: the man will hear Johnny's mockery; should she run or apologize? But then, so quickly that on a first viewing it is difficult to absorb the events in their full significance, the man lurches forward to attack them, kills Johnny and is clawing after Barbara as she runs screaming to the car. She gets the door shut and then finds she has no ignition key, as her pursuer's distorted features leer against the glass. Finally she lets the brake off and runs the car down the hill, reaching a small farmhouse, where she moves from room to room, desperately trying to escape her pursuer.

As with Hitchcock in *Psycho*, Romero has no intention of allowing his audience to slip into an easy state of identification with his heroine. She carries us through the first few riveting minutes of the film, but now, with a psychological verisimilitude which is again unexpected, she subsides into a state of total shock, which can only increase as the activities and intentions of the flesh-eating corpses become clearer. Her life is saved by Ben, a black fugitive from the chaos outside the house. His practical resourcefulness, as he struggles to create a sanctuary

against the undead, exactly parallels the survival instinct of Matheson's hero in *I Am Legend* who manifests the same rationality in the face of total social breakdown. Soon the pair are joined by the Cooper family, parents and daughter, who have barricaded themselves in the cellar, together with a young teenage couple, Tom and Judy. But conflict breaks out when Harry Cooper, a reactionary bigot, evidently loathed by his wife, challenges Ben's strategy and insists on staying down in the cellar, where their little girl is ill from a wound inflicted by one of the corpses.

By this stage the undead are besieging the house, and their appearance is harrowing, because they seem to represent a cross-section of the dead community, the random outpouring of the local morgue and cemetery. There are the young in dirty shrouds, old men in tattered overalls, a naked woman with an identity tag on her arm, bloody-mouthed accident victims, even skeletal children. They seem like the lost inhabitants of a forgotten land, returning to remind the living of their existence. Only their staring expressionless faces and scrabbling moaning gestures connect them with each other.

A portable television informs the house's occupants that the undead appear to have been animated by some stray radiation from a returning Venus probe. They can be destroyed by fire or bullets to the brain, and normal scruples should be put aside: it is a natural disaster not Armageddon. The announcer's brutal logic establishes the central tension on which the film rests, because its practical assertiveness blindly contradicts our perception of the horrors that are unfolding. And reservations about his tone are borne out by events. The living dead stage a massive assault on the house during which the little Cooper girl, who is now one of them, proceeds to attack and eat her parents. Helen Cooper dies because she proves unable to set emotion aside and retaliate against her child. Meanwhile, Ben's escape plan has resulted in the teenage couple being burned

Below centre and bottom: Judy, the teenage girl, tends the sick child in the basement of the house, and later makes a desperate attempt to escape the ghouls.

Below and top left: The strangely varied ghouls surround the lonely house in Romero's *Night of the Living Dead.* Most of the actors were chosen from the local community.

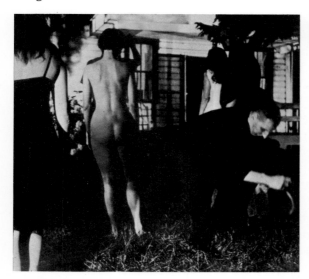

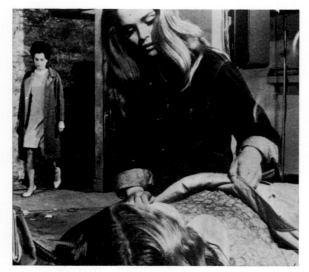

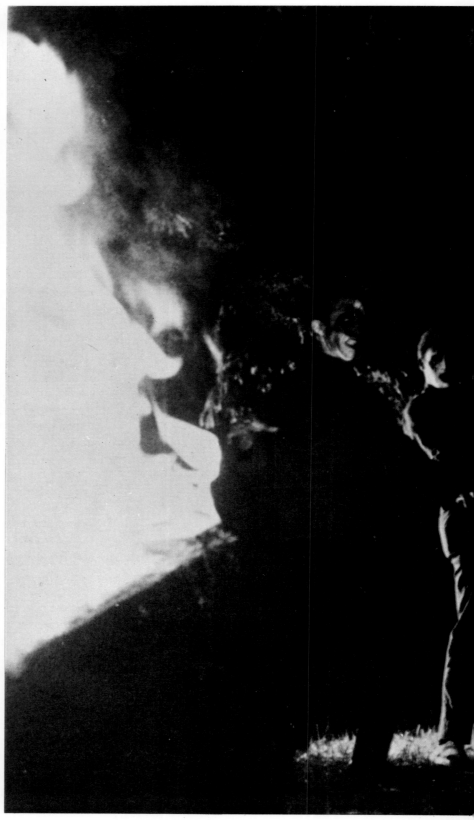

alive and eaten while Barbara, who had recovered some composure, is destroyed when her brother, now one of the undead, appears at the door.

Finally, only Ben is left barricaded in the cellar, and the whole perspective of the film now drastically switches to a huge search-and-destroy operation being conducted by the local Sheriff and his posse. Their complacent jargon as they move through the landscape, shooting and burning, immediately invokes similar operations in south-east Asia. 'They go up pretty easy,' says the Sheriff with satisfaction as another writhing body is immolated. These men are ridding the countryside of cannibalistic ghouls, but Romero presents their activities in such a way that it is impossible to feel relief.

Instead, we have moved from one kind of living death to another, the ghouls who killed for food manifested more natural qualities than the posse's crude indifference, a total obliviousness to the ghastly environment through which they are walking, surrounded by dogs and helicopters and radios. Ben hears the rescue party and emerges from the cellar where he has been hiding. As he appears at the door, one of the posse shoots him casually in the head. '*Good* shot,' says the Sheriff.

It seems in no way surprising that American International Pictures rejected the film for distribution purely because of the ending's impact. It is the subversive centre of the whole, because it immediately equates the horrors we have seen with a recognizable and relevant aspect of contemporary reality. Without ever departing from its enormously exciting narrative development or making any reference outside its subject matter, *Night of the Living Dead* manages to bring us closer to the psychological underpinnings of war, especially racist war, than many of the recent documentaries which have tackled such subjects directly. The unhappy ending now became almost universal in horror movies, but more importantly *Night of the Living Dead* broadened the whole genre's frame of reference, redirecting our attention to a more general and political reading of the vampire myth than anyone had thought possible.

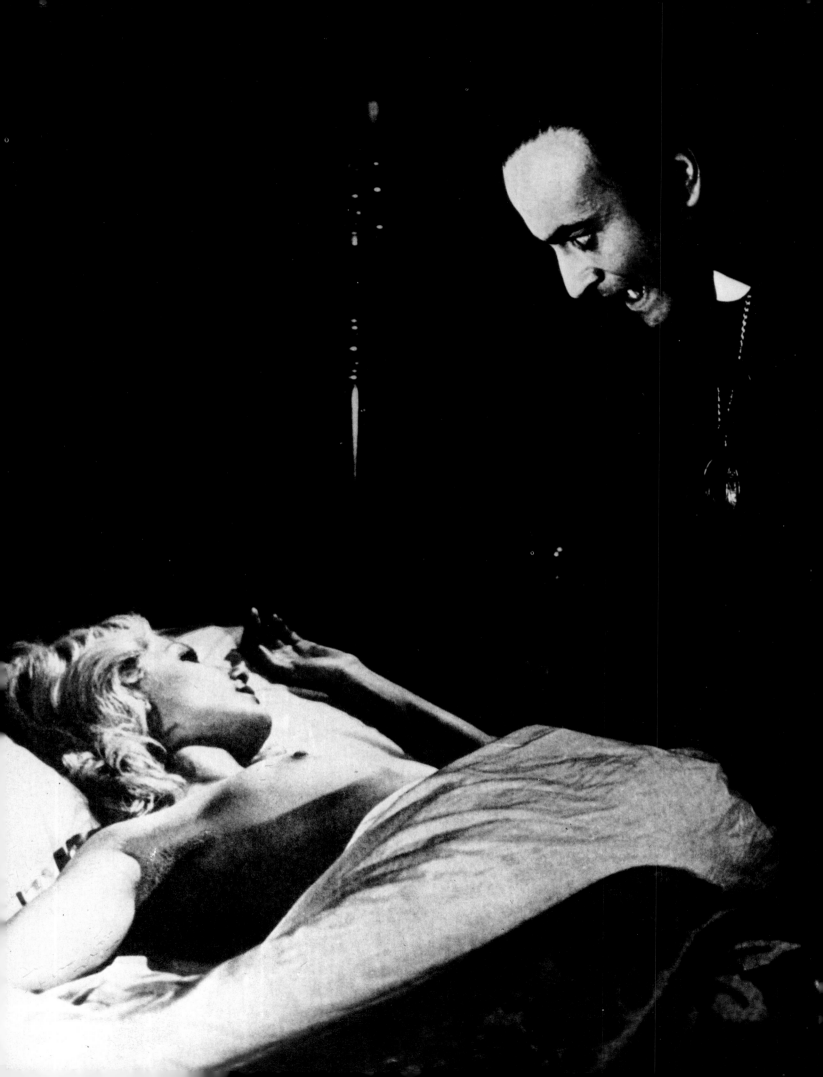

THE LATIN VAMPIRE

'The blood is the life!'

Paul Naschy in one of his very few ferocious moments in the sentimental *El Gran Amor del Conde Dracula.*

THE POPULARITY of the vampire theme in Latin countries was recognized as early as 1931, when Universal shot a Spanish-speaking version of *Dracula* on the sets of the Lugosi original with the American George Melford directing. This was at a time when the problem of translating sound films had not been completely thought out, and such an elaborate precaution was thought to protect the international investment. Unfortunately the film is utterly lost, and we lack even a written record from someone who saw it. But Carlos Villarias, who played the title role, was to be the first in a long line of Spanish screen vampires, and in some ways his sleek good looks made him better suited to the part than Lugosi.

It seems reasonable to suppose that audiences with a Roman Catholic background are more likely to be receptive to the idea of spiritual evil and its associated manifestations. Perhaps, through the Catholic emphasis on the Mass, they have a greater response towards any ritual surrounding blood. There is also a kind of operatic quality about the vampire myth and its subject, which relates it to the Spanish legend of Don Juan, the cruel and impious lover. Not surprisingly, the creator of the first Gothic vampire, Lord Byron, identified with Don Juan, making him the hero of one of his most famous poems.

Of all the Latin countries, Mexico has probably produced the greatest number of fantasy films, but there are serious difficulties involved in comparing its 'vampire' films with those of other countries. The Mexican cinema operates for an entirely different cultural market than its American or European counter-part, and its approach to genre material is correspondingly different. The hardcore popular cinema it produces serves less as linear narrative than as spectacle, involving the endless repetition of certain familiar fictional conventions. A typical example is the Santo series, which involves a masked wrestler El Santo (literally the Saint) whose numerous films are built around a series of unending wrestling matches with all the heavies of western folklore from Frankenstein and Dracula through to Jack the Ripper, Hitler and even

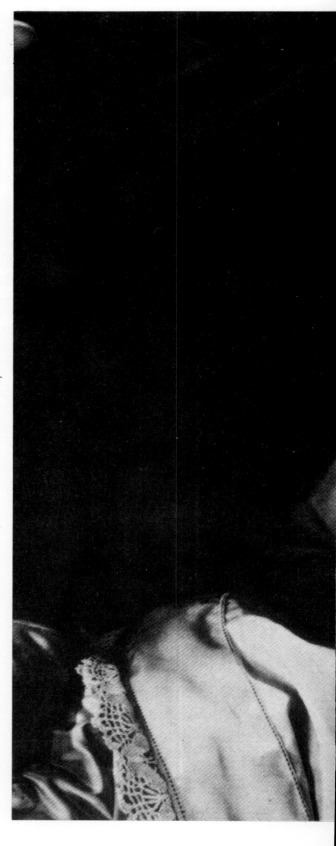

The other Universal Dracula: Carlos Villarias vampirizes Carmen Guerrero in a Spanish-speaking version of Stoker's novel, shot on the sets of the Lugosi original.

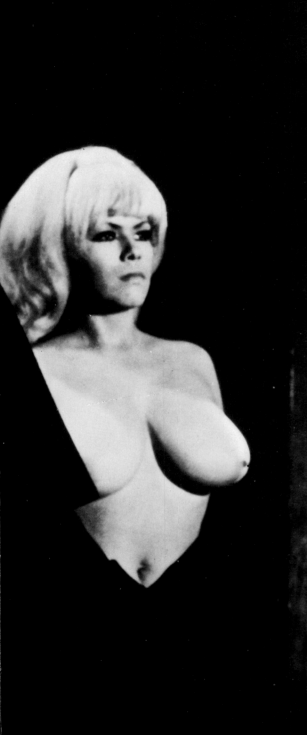

Satan himself. To itemize the narrative of these films would be pointless and even patronizing, without taking time out to consider them in a proper cultural perspective. But it's worth noting that the Mexican movie audience have had at least two series which have some affinity to the Dracula cycle. The first, inaugurated strangely in 1957, the same year as Hammer's *Dracula*, was *El Vampiro* with German Robles as the vampire Count Lavud.

Despite the misty Gothic trappings Lavud was a modern-day vampire in the Latin operatic mould. He returned soon afterwards in *El Ataud del Vampiro*, where the presence of a mad scientist and a wax museum reflects the picaresue but frequently baffling abandon with which Mexican film-makers mix their plots and styles. The ending of *El Ataud* (US title: *The Vampire's Coffin*) was also novel in that Lavud was impaled against a wall, while still in the form of a bat, by a thrown spear.

Lavud gave way to a far more complex vampire hero called Nostradamus, who is revealed in *La Maldicion de Nostradamus* (US title: *Curse of Nostradamus*) to be the son of the sixteenth-century astrologer Michael Nostradamus. Battling with a Van Helsing figure called Professor Dolenz and intent on destroying the whole world if necessary, Nostradamus kept going for four films, concentrating mainly on vampire-type killing and possession, though he did once try to create an eclipse of the sun.

In Spain itself, the horror cinema seems to have got properly under way by about 1961

Aldo Monti plays Dracula in *Santo en el Tesoro de Dracula*, one of the seemingly endless series of films about the Mexican masked wrestler who is pitted against every conceivable human and supernatural villain. Santo's surrealist adventures are continually juxtaposed with his activities in the wrestling ring.

German Robles, one of
the earliest Mexican
vampires, as the elegant
Count Lavud in *El
Vampiro.*

with the continuing popular success of the Dr. Orloff series, inaugurated by *The Horrible Dr. Orloff*, a sub-Frankenstein monster picture. Its director Jess Franco has subsequently veered between standard softcore exploitation and more fantastic subjects, but he has rarely explored the vampire theme. In fact, vampirism only became a prolific film subject in Spain towards the end of the 1960s, and Franco, whose work tends very much towards international co-production, very often gave his vampire movies a sex orientation: *Vampyros Lesbos* in 1971 was a German/Spanish co-production, with Paul Müller and Dennis Price, in which an American girl is haunted by a beautiful woman who turns out to be a descendant of Count Dracula. Franco frequently writes his own scripts for these quickly made but always widely distributed movies, and he claimed that this one was based on Stoker's short story *Dracula's Guest*, but the connection is difficult to establish.

The same year Franco persuaded Howard Vernon to play Count Dracula in the rubbishy *Dracula contra el Doctor Frankenstein* and followed it with *La Hija de Dracula* in 1972 in which Vernon is again surrounded by a predictable amount of naked flesh. Much more interesting was Franco's earlier *Succubus*, sometimes known as *Dreamed Sins* or *Necronomicon* (although it has no connection with H. P. Lovecraft's mythical occult book of the same name) in which a girl night-club entertainer, who specializes in the simulation of sadistic acts, is goaded by the erotic taunts of a demonic stranger. Finally its central character seems to have entered a total fantasy world.

Franco attempted a straight adaptation of Stoker in 1970. Christopher Lee agreed to star in *El Conde Dracula* on condition that it would be a faithful reconstruction of the original. Its credits announce that 'Now for the first time we tell it exactly as Stoker wrote it', but even in the first few minutes the invention of a new character, as Harker travels by train to Bistritz, does not bode well. As night falls

Christopher Lee in Jess Franco's unsuccessful attempt to recreate Bram Stoker's portrayal of Dracula.

during the coach-ride to Castle Dracula, the day-for-night photography is dismally shoddy. Christopher Lee's appearance as the Count, with drooping moustache and cruel pale features, comes close to a physical approximation of Stoker's character, and the film seems to have been shot in an authentic castle.

For some reason Franco presents his Dracula with an almost funereal dullness, abandoning all the captivating energy and intelligence described in the novel. He also substitutes for the 'well lighted and warmed' rooms which Stoker describes, a huge austere mausoleum where the two eat in near-darkness.

In fact the Count is presented with so little animation that even when he is rescuing Harker from the attentions of the vampire women, he looks barely preoccupied. The almost comical under-acting scarcely compares with Harker's comments in the book that 'never did I imagine such wrath and fury, even to the demons of the pit. His eyes were positively blazing.' As the film progresses, its token attempts at authenticity are progressively whittled away: instead of climbing down the wall of Castle Dracula, Harker jumps headlong over the side, and then wakes up in Van Helsing's clinic in a Victorian England which is obviously modern Spain.

It picks up again briefly with a few good scenes involving Klaus Kinski as the lunatic Renfield (probably the best Renfield the cinema

has yet presented) but the action soon becomes a terribly static working out of the story's most elementary aspects. Lucy's death-scene for example, which ranked as one of the novel's highlights, marking the lowest ebb in the struggle against Dracula, sinks to a depth of bathos here that has barely been èqualled, even in the coarsest vampire production: 'She's dead,' someone tells Herbert Lom's Van Helsing. 'It is a sign', he replies with fatuous complacency. 'Perhaps it is not too late for me to act.'

Miserably constructed as a thriller, in spite of (or because of) the fact that it boasts no less than five writers, Franco's *El Conde Dracula* probably did more disservice to the Dracula character than the cheapest of his sexploitation movies. At least they make no claim to be definitive.

A number of other non-Dracula vampire films have been made in Spain during the 1970s, and some of them have attempted to explore new aspects of the theme. Among the most interesting was *Tomb of the Blind Dead* (*Noche del Terror Ciego*, 1972), partly inspired by *Night of the Living Dead*, in which a girl on a camping holiday leaves her erring boyfriend to take a look at a deserted monastery, and witnesses a massive eruption of skeletal ghouls with plucked-out eyes. They turn out to be the remains of devil-worshipping Templars who were executed at the time of the Crusade. After the girl's body is found sucked dry of blood, the film settles down to a more mundane level of suspicion and counter-suspicion, but it revives when the Knights Templars take to horse and swarm aboard a train, creating havoc amongst the passengers. The image of a massive invasion of the undead, which cannot only obstruct, but obliterate, the modern world, is as powerful as ever, and the film spawned a sequel by the same director, Amando de Osorio, *El Ataque de los Muertos Sin Ojos* in 1973.

Probably the best-known specialist in Spanish horror is Paul Naschy, whose affection for the Universal style has brought the same streak of weird pathos to a whole series of Gothic films. His principal character is a woebegone werewolf who began life in *La Marca del Hombre*

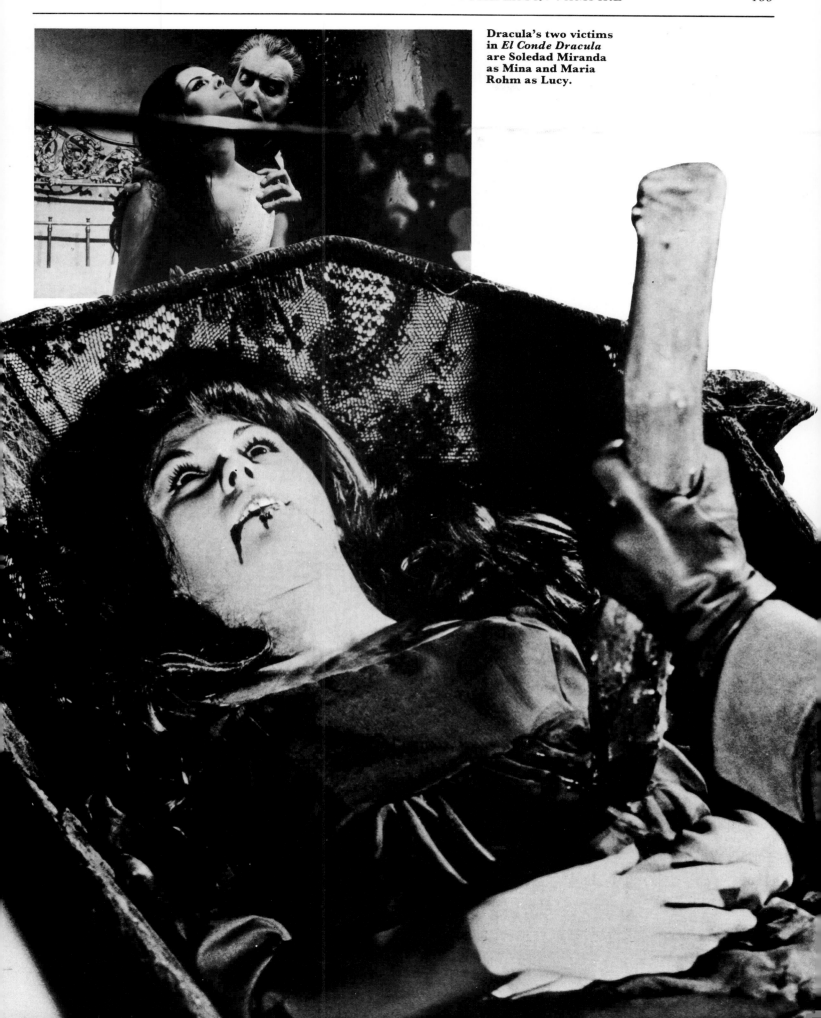

Dracula's two victims in *El Conde Dracula* are Soledad Miranda as Mina and Maria Rohm as Lucy.

Lobo (*Frankenstein's Bloody Terror*, 1969), but Naschy himself has not matched quantity with quality in the numerous films that followed. Stocky and rather flat as an actor, his enthusiasm is occasionally conveyed by odd touches of originality and most of his work has the advantage of firm direction from the Spanish horror veteran Leon Klimovsky (without Naschy, Klimovsky put together a few other vampire pictures like the offbeat *Saga of the Draculas*, 1972, in which an aged Count is desperately trying to find a way to continue his line).

Probably Naschy's most interesting achievement is his bizarre resurrection of the Countess Bathory in *Werewolf Versus the Vampire Woman* (*La Noche de Walpurgis*, 1970). Bathory is revived accidentally by two thesis-writing students and immediately becomes a suitable foe for the lovable werewolf hero who is throughout the series pitted against various vampire villains. The Countess made another appearance in *El Retorno de Walpurgis* (this time directed by Carlos Aured). But Naschy's rather maudlin approach to the Gothic has not served him well in his attempts to make proper Dracula movies: *El Gran Amor del Conde Dracula* is a mawkish and uneventful film with a highly histrionic Dracula.

The only Latin country to develop a horror cinema with international critical recognition is Italy. The Italian epics of the 1950s and 1960s, which won international box-office success with the unending Hercules series from 1957, had frequently incorporated Gothic elements. Surprisingly perhaps, these films also proved an extremely fruitful nursery of talent for some of Italy's most promising directors, writers and technicians. Michelangelo Antonioni himself had worked as an uncredited co-director on *Sign of the Gladiator*, in 1958. The second unit director on that picture was Riccardo Freda, a cultured and imaginative film-maker who, as early as two years previously in 1956, had put together a vampire movie *I Vampiri* (US title: *The Devil's Commandment*; British title: *Lust of the Vampire*).

Set in Paris, the film is a striking variation on the Bathory story about an old Duchess who has been using the blood of young women in order to adopt the persona of her beautiful niece Giselle. Gianno-Maria Canale is the Duchess Marguerite and Dario Michaelis plays the reporter hero. Although pedestrian by modern standards, the film was daringly original in its time, especially in its straight equation of blood and sex.

Before entering films, Riccardo Freda had been a sculptor, a newspaper art critic and teacher. He was one of the first to appreciate the enormous possibilities of the Gothic style for Italian movies, and he drew on his training as an artist to create a vigorous expressionist colour approach to horror which was partly inspired by Hammer, but developed into something quite original. In his eclectic career Freda practised almost every conceivable cinematic genre, but he claims to have found horror the most intricate of all the popular movie forms, because of the difficult range of emotions it generates in audiences.

His main contribution to the genre is exemplified by the two Dr. Hitchcock films, *The Horrible Secret of Dr. Hitchcock* and *The Ghost* (both 1962). Set in a beautifully lurid version of nineteenth-century London, only the

Mario Bava's amalgamation of SF and vampirism on a tiny budget: *Planet of the Vampires*.

ANITA EKBERG • JOHN HAMILTON • DIANA LORYS DANS

MALENKA
LA VAMPIRE

EASTMANCOLOR   UNE PRODUCTION

MISE EN SCÈNE DE
AMANDO DE OSSORIO

Si vous n'avez pas peur de Dracula, ni des monstres de Frankenstein, si les châteaux hantés et les vampires ne vous impressionnent pas... venez voir le film de JESS FRANCO

Cocinor présente

DENNIS PRICE ● HOWARD VERNON ● ANNE UBERT

DRACULA prisonnier de FRANKENSTEIN

UN FILM DE JESS FRANCO

Cocinor

first has slight undertones of vampirism, but they were remarkably influential both in their accumulation of a subtly uncanny atmosphere and in the employment of an actress, who was to do as much for the female vampire as Christopher Lee had done for Dracula, the English émigrée Barbara Steele.

Freda has talked of Steele's eyes as 'metaphysical, impossible, they are the eyes of a Chirico painting. Sometimes in certain lighting conditions, her face takes on expressions which don't seem human, and would be impossible for any other actress.' It was a strange transformation for a girl from Birkenhead, who had been discovered by the Rank Organisation doing rep at the Citizen's Theatre, Glasgow. Rank had proceeded to bury her in a series of

films like *Bachelor of Hearts* and *Upstairs and Downstairs*, until one of her English films attracted the attention of the leading director of Italian fantasy cinema, Mario Bava.

Bava had been drawn into films through his father, a sculptor, who had been called up by Pathé one memorable night in 1906 to sculpt a coffin door for a silent movie. Bava's father went on to become a notable silent cameraman and Bava himself (who attaches great symbolic significance to the coffin-door episode) became a movie addict. Later he went on to become a major cinematographer himself, working on numerous early epics including the Hercules series.

On more than one occasion Bava was forced to direct part of these films himself, and in 1956, he worked as cameraman to Freda on *I Vampiri*. In the middle of shooting, Freda had a quarrel with the producers and Bava had to finish the film in two days (the entire schedule was only twelve shooting days), including a long sequence of the Paris streets which was actually shot in the old garden of a Roman house. Even at this stage Bava was fascinated by the possibilities of the macabre. Unlike so many former cameramen driven into the horror field by circumstance, it is Bava's favourite cinematic form. In an interview with the Spanish magazine *Terror Fantastic*, he talks of the horrific ingredients of his dreams: 'My dreams are always horrible . . . there's a character that continuously haunts me in my nightmares, he's a musician that serenades his lover with a violin, strung with the nerves of his own arm.'

Not surprisingly, when he was offered the chance to direct his own movie in 1960, Bava picked out Barbara Steele as the star, and around her he built one of the most haunting (yet mythologically confused) vampire films the cinema has yet seen. *Mask of the Demon* (also: *Revenge of the Vampire* or *Black Sunday*) is loosely based on Gogol's short story *The Vij*. Barbara Steele plays the witch Asa who, together with her lover, is condemned by the

Russian Inquisition in the Middle Ages to be put to death by a spiked mask which is hammered onto her face. In 1830, two travellers en route to Moscow, Andrej (John Richardson) and Chomar (Andrea Checchi) come upon her sarcophagus and remove the mask to reveal the rotted remnants of the sorceress's features. Owing to the accidental spilling of Chomar's blood, Asa is slowly revived and, together with her resurrected lover, they proceed to terrorize the isolated castle community in a variety of grisly ways until he finds a manuscript which explains how to exorcize the witch.

If ever a horror film was pure style it is *Mask of the Demon*. It is the only one of Bava's films which justifies the charge that he favours atmosphere over plot. The basic story is an unpromising hybrid which succumbs very much to formula, with Barbara Steele playing the resurrected sorceress as well as her modern descendant Katia. But the impact of the finished film is so drastic that it was banned outright in many countries for much of the 1960s.

Bava shoots in a compelling monochrome style, making the utmost of the gloomy sets, the exotic settings and of Steele herself. It was the film that first brought her to international attention; the stark and horrifying image of her as the rematerialized witch, with eyes broad and staring, and ghastly spike marks neatly penetrating the milk-pale skin, remains especially memorable. Unfortunately the English version of *Mask of the Demon* was devastated by dubbing which sounds as though it belongs, not just to a different film, but to a different world from the near-hysterical images on the screen. American International also added a ghastly Les Baxter score (the original Italian music was by Roberto Nicolosi). But even this devastation could not prevent the film from accumulating a legendary reputation.

As the Italian horror field got underway, English pseudonyms began to appear on the films' credit titles. Contrary to popular belief, this was originally not so much for export as for the home market. Riccardo Freda had conceived the idea in the late fifties, when he came across a cinema in San Remo showing *I Vampiri*. Freda was keen to assess his film's audience impact but found the cinema virtually empty. Back outside, he watched the potential customers go by. The advertising for the film was good, and the subject caught people's attention. But as Freda stood there, several Italians were put off when they caught sight of his name as director. They were convinced that no Italian could make a horror film, and therefore it would not be worth the price of admission. Doubly determined to break the English and American monopoly, Freda hit upon the idea of making his horror movies under the name Robert Hampton, and he was copied by scores of other film-makers.

Mario Bava adopted the name John M. Old, and under it he proceeded to make a whole series of horror films, which have rightly secured his reputation as one of the masters in the field. In the minutely budgeted *La Frustra e il Corpo*, (British title: *Night is the Phantom*; US title: *What!*) he obtained one of Christopher Lee's most remarkable performances as the demonic spectre of a woman's sadistic lover who has returned to haunt her. Bava leaves the psychological dimension of the plot open (so that it is never quite clear whether Lee is the figment of an erotic nightmare or a real ghost) and incorporates a wealth of sexual association into the story. The film's comparative success makes it more regrettable than ever that Bava never worked on a Dracula movie (he had previously collaborated with Lee on the semi-vampiric *Hercules in the Centre of the Earth* two years earlier in 1961).

Bava was responsible for an ingenious cut-price science-fiction movie with a vampire theme, *Planet of the Vampires*, but probably his most influential Gothic approach to the subject was in the excellent multi-episode Boris Karloff film *Black Sabbath* (*I Tre Volti della Paura*, 1963). Like *Mask of the Demon* this was again set in nineteenth-century Russia, and was

One of the great neo-Gothic vampire movies, *Mask of the Demon*, shot in a compelling monochrome style: Barbara Steele inaugurated her career as *the* female horror cult figure, playing a medieval witch who is resurrected in the 19th century. The grisly Inquisition torture sequence was partly responsible for the film's rough treatment at the hands of the censorship authorities.

The later Italian horror films with Barbara Steele: as a lesbian vampire in *La Danza Macabra* (left), and as the vengeful ghost in *Long Hair of Death* (right).

Opposite: **A French poster for a Jess Franco spin-off.**

based on a Russian short story, *The Wurdalak* by Tolstoy.

The chilling construction of *The Wurdalak* initiated certain themes that were to be a strong feature of many later vampire films. A traveller riding across the Russian wastes comes upon a headless corpse, and then a family who are anxiously awaiting the return of their father Gorka. He has informed them that if he does not return before sunset on the fifth day, then he must be destroyed as the undead. In the event, just as the sun is falling, the father arrives home. He is played with gaunt brilliance by Karloff himself (who has narrated the rest of the film). The family greet him in the hope that he is unharmed, but there is a disquieting atmosphere as they eat supper. Finally after dinner, Gorka makes a grab for his grandchild, and the rest of the film sees the gradual dismemberment of the whole family, including an agonizing scene which looks forward to *Night of the Living Dead* where a child, now one of the undead, is beating on its mother's door, begging to be let in from the cold.

As always, Bava's style here is impeccable. The studio exteriors have a resplendent, eerie beauty while an ice-cold blue aura surrounds the father, returning in the transmuted form of a vampire. But unlike so many other cameramen who have graduated to directing horror (Freddie Francis is the obvious example), Bava has, since *Mask of the Demon*, generally avoided relying on stylistic effects to boost vapid plots. His style is worked out in direct relation to his film's subjects, and he particularly seems to favour thematic constructions which blur the borderline between reality on the one hand and dream or psychosis

on the other. Since the early sixties, much of his finest horror work has centred on the examination of various psychoses like the astonishing *Blood Brides* (*Un Hacha para la Luna de Miel*). He has rarely been daunted by the tiny budgets with which he works.

Meanwhile, much to her own frustration, Barbara Steele had been fixed forever in the popular imagination as either a terrorized victim or an avenging sex-vampire, and frequently both. In Freda's two Hitchcock films she had played each role, and in Antonio Margheriti's *Long Hair of Death* (*Lunghi Capelli della Morte*, 1964) she is a suspected killer who is burned alive and returns to exact a harrowing revenge. Occasionally, usually in order to exploit masochistic possibilities, her blood is found to be necessary for the rejuvenation of a madman's earlier love, notably Freda's *Horrible Secret* and Caiano's *Amanti d'Oltretomba* (US title: *Nightmare Castle*; British title: *The Faceless Monster*).

One of the rare occasions on which she played an orthodox vampire who is actually seen to suck blood was Antonio Margheriti's *La Danza Macabra*, 1963, supposedly based on a short story by Poe. In fact it was a totally fictitious concoction involving Steele as a lesbian vampire some years before this trend became fashionable in horror cinema, and the comparative audacity of the material caused production problems. At one point, according to Barbara Steele's own amusing account in *Midi-Minuit Fantastique*, Margaret Robsham, who was married to the Italian actor Ugo Tognazzi, utterly refused to kiss her, though it was vital for the scene. Margheriti was finally driven to screaming at her, 'Pretend it's Ugo, forget Barbara.' Somehow it's difficult to take

BRITT NICHOLS
ANNE LIBERT
ALBERT DALBES
présente
DANS

LA FILLE DE DRACULA

the erotic content seriously, after imagining this episode.

Very rapidly Barbara Steele became a kind of popular icon, invoking images of evil sensuality and cruelty, and (less often) terrified submission whenever she appeared. As her fame spread, her artistic ambitions grew and soon she was only prepared to provide quick cameos in horror movies which would involve as little time as possible.

The late Michael Reeves, one of England's most remarkable young directors before he died in 1969, made this kind of use of Steele in the amusing *Revenge of the Bloodbeast* which, in its tremendous opening, emulated the style of *Mask of the Demon*. But by this time, she seems to have become extremely disillusioned with her career as an actress, and her appear-

ances became increasingly rare. Mario Bava maintains that she was side-tracked by her role in Fellini's *8½* and became fixated with the idea of only making intellectual films, which nobody would offer her. There was, however, a certain justification in her complaint that the kind of films she made were a lot more fun for their directors than for the cast. And finally she moved to America where one of her last parts was the prison warden in *Caged Heat*.

There were other genre horror stars in Italy, notably Walter Brandi, who presided over a succession of girlie vampire pictures. But none even approached the quality of sensual cinematic mystery that so many talented filmmakers had been able to develop with Barbara Steele. The strange fact that she was English, yet became indubitably an *Italian*

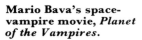

Mario Bava's space-vampire movie, *Planet of the Vampires*.

movie star, reflects partly on the inadequacy of the British film industry in the fifties and partly on the increasing internationalism of film production. As the 1970s got underway, and England joined the Common Market, it was becoming increasingly difficult to distinguish the product of one European industry from another. And the confusion is demonstrated by two recent vampire films.

Joseph Larraz's *Vampyres* and Jorge Grau's *Living Dead at the Manchester Morgue* are the twin poles of the vampire cinema as they exist at present. The former is an effectively cloying and yet nihilistic story of two lesbian succubi. The latter is an accomplished remake of Romero's *Night of the Living Dead*.

Vampyres was made in 1974 by the painter Joseph Larraz who first worked in Britain at the beginning of the 1970s, and attracted attention with the superb psychological thriller *Symptoms* (a British entry at Cannes). *Vampyres* was much more of a straight exploitation film than its predecessor, concentrating obsessively on a steadily intensified sexual claustrophobia. It begins with two lesbian lovers, Fran and Miriam (Marianna Morris and Anulka) being shot dead in the bedroom of an old manor house by an unknown assailant. The girls become sex vampires and leave their graves at night to lure motorists to the crumbling old mansion.

One of their victims, Ted (Murray Brown), proves so appealing to Fran that after a night of sex and vampirism he is not sucked dry of blood like all the others but left in the house at daybreak. Weak from loss of blood and infatuated with Fran, Ted stays to become weaker and weaker after each nocturnal bout. Soon he can hardly move at all, but briefly manages to stagger out into the garden where he attracts the attention of two campers. Finally as the victims accumulate around him, he manages to alert the couple in the caravan. But before they can drive him to the hospital the couple are viciously attacked and murdered by the vampires. The next morning Ted wakes up, half-delirious in his car, as an estate agent impresses his naive American clients with the house's 'ghost story'.

It is a minimal plot, but Larraz manages to play on its fairytale monotony to accumulate an atmosphere of bloody eroticism, which resembles the cruder episodes of the *Arabian Nights*. With feverish insistence, the vampirism is graphically incorporated into the sex act itself and at one point the vampire girl is seen literally prising her gorged partner from the drained body of her lover and tottering in a kind of blood inebriation towards the cellar as daylight approaches. If *Vampyres* is interesting, it is because it takes the idea of sex vampirism about as far as it can go, in terms of the satiated sensual exhaustion the film conveys. The absence of any real plot, apart from Ted's gradual slide into total physical debility as a result of each nocturnal bout, only adds to this overall impression.

In contrast, *The Living Dead at the Manchester Morgue* suggests fresh possibilities for the vampire movie by building on the ideas of its extraordinary prototype. It begins with the hero riding out of London on his motorbike on what seems like a normal day. But the rapid montage of dead birds, belching diesel fumes and oblivious human faces soon suggests a landscape that is unaccountably dying. This is confirmed by the radio newscast warning against 'hysteria when confronted with ecological problems, many of them exaggerated'. A chance accident forces the boy to hitch a lift with a girl, who seems nervous, and they get lost on an eerie stretch of farmroad. The boy walks up to a lonely farmhouse to ask the way, as if the film was going to develop into the standard maniac-at-large plot. He sees an odd white machine manned by two simple-minded yet enthusiastic technicians, who explain that its radiation is highly effective in pest control. Meanwhile, back at the car, the girl is being threatened by a gaunt bearded man, with all the pallor of a newly revived corpse. The farmer recognizes his description as that of an itinerant tramp who has just been buried.

Now the incidences of violence begin to multiply. They arrive at a cottage to find the girl's brother-in-law has been viciously murdered, but there is no evidence to suggest who or why. A brutal, anti-permissive police inspector suspects them both, but when the boy visits a local hospital he finds that newly-born babies are inflicting bloody bite-wounds on their nurses and mothers. The doctor explains that the condition is recent and the boy unsuccessfully attempts to connect it with the pest control machine.

Later the couple decide to visit a nearby churchyard to look for the body of the man she has · seen, and they are trapped in a vault by the living dead, who have already eaten the churchwarden. It appears that they transmit life to each other through the blood of the living – like a plague. The couple only escape when they discover that fire can destroy the undead (exactly like their predecessors in Romero's film).

From now on, the film records the couple's paranoid flight from the undead and the police who suspect them of 'black magic' killing. The blind stupidity of the authorities eventually ensures that the heroine is incarcerated in the hospital with dozens of flesh-devouring corpses, while the hero is under arrest. He manages to escape and destroy the undead by setting fire to the hospital, but the police shoot him dead as he completes his work. Later, in all ignorance of what he has done, the complacent detective returns to his hotel room basking in the plaudits of the press and his superiors (who believe he has saved the countryside from a couple of psychopathic kids). But the living corpse of the hero is there to destroy him.

As will be seen from this synopsis, *Living Dead at the Manchester Morgue* is as ambiguous as *Night of the Living Dead* in its attitude to the monsters it portrays. Like the earlier film, it ultimately identifies the hero with the undead

The two voracious lesbian vampires from Joseph Larraz's recent film *Vampyres* : Fran (Marianne Morris) is the blonde vampire who falls unexpectedly in love with one of her victims. Miriam (Anulka) is her partner.

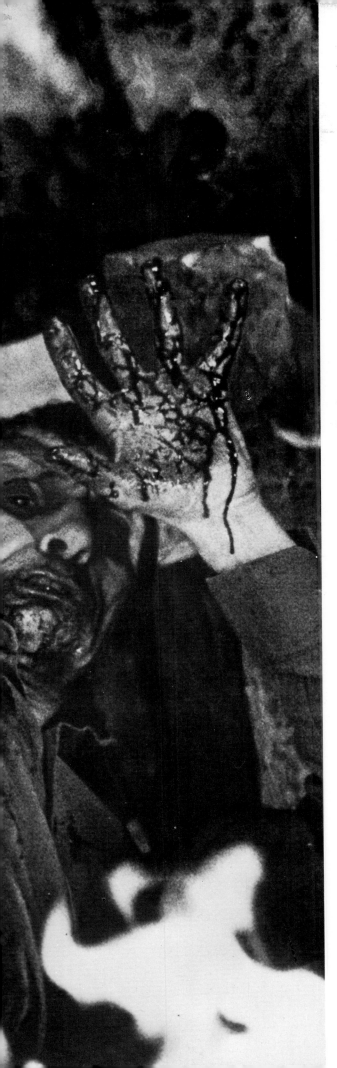

Three representatives of _The Living Dead at the Manchester Morgue_, a compellingly apocalyptic study of mass vampirism shot on location in northern England by a Spanish-Italian production unit.

rather than the forces of law and order. But Grau takes matters a stage further by actually permitting his hero to become a vampire on the side of justice. The audience is easily persuaded to sympathize with his final revenge on the detective, who has persecuted him throughout the action and been instrumental in causing the tragedy. Of course the twist involves a blatant inconsistency, because the film has never previously suggested that the undead retain any human intelligence at all. They are the machine-like product of radiation sickness. But the climax is still effective.

The Living Dead at the Manchester Morgue is certainly more opportunistic than its predecessor, and the repeated coincidences, which always just prevent the policeman from discovering the truth, strain its credibility almost to breaking point. But, given these lapses in construction, there is no doubt that Grau has grasped the essential possibilities of his theme. The sequence in the vault as the couple scramble to get their legs up a ventilation hole out of reach of the scrabbling, shuffling undead below is classically effective, as is the gradual accumulation of uneasy detail in the first twenty minutes. The characters' bewilderment at being confronted by a mythical threat in a modern context ('We have to defend ourselves.' 'What with? Silver bullets or a wooden stake?') sometimes jars, but is fortunately given less emphasis than the sense of apocalypse which seems to be such an indispensable component of the new social approach to fantasy.

Films like _The Living Dead at the Manchester Morgue_ are not by any means a trite return to the science fiction vampires of the 1950s. By fusing the theme of contemporary social breakdown with the more Freudian and individual terror of Gothic fiction, they extend the horror field into a new and more viable area that could be loosely termed the cinema of Gothic anxiety. The fact that this enterprising remake of Romero was a Spanish/Italian co-production suggests that the Latin cinema may be at present more prepared than its English counterpart to break away from the mundane repetition of overworked themes.

CONCLUSION

The new German
cinema has not entirely
ignored its own heri-
tage of horror; Heinz
Geissendorfer's
*Jonathan, Vampire
Sterben Nicht* portrays
Dracula in a political
light as a sadistic
Hitler figure.

UNFORTUNATELY even the more creative of the new vampire movies have not met with the commercial success they deserve. *Night of the Living Dead* made a considerable amount of money in some countries, including America, but its business career was marred by a tangle of litigation between producer and distributor. *Manchester Morgue* does not seen to have met with much public response (perhaps because of its stale lookalike title). And, worst of all, Willard Huyck's *Messiah of Evil* (*The Second Coming*), a brilliant movie which exceeds virtually every other Gothic horror film since the war in terms of narrative ingenuity, has had no release whatsoever since its screening out of competition at the Cannes festival in 1974.

The burial of Huyck's film, an extraordinary evocation of the world of H. P. Lovecraft set in a mysterious American coastal town, is probably the most depressing thing that could happen to the vampire cinema. Because it suggests that the field has declined to such an extent that quality and originality no longer have any significance. The film was packed with classic sequences: the girl tentatively exploring a bright and empty supermarket where she suddenly discovers the customers crowded around the freezer, consuming raw meat; the chase in which she finally manages to hitch a lift from a passing lorry-driver who seems normal until he picks a live rodent out of his pocket and casually bites its head off; the sequence in the local cinema where an unsuspecting girl watches a strange western from a deserted auditorium as the undead slowly surround her. If a vampire movie like this cannot obtain distribution, then it is hard to see how the form has any real possibility of development. On the other hand, *Messiah of Evil* may simply be subject to one of those inexplicable delays that still seem to dog independent distributors.

There have been a few attempts (also unseen by the great majority of audiences) to try and bring the Count himself into the new thematic trend in vampire cinema. *Jonathan, Vampire Sterben Nicht*, written and directed in Germany by Hans W. Geissendorfer portrays Dracula as a ranting and sadistic Hitler-figure

Poster for *Le Nosferat*, a stylized Brechtian reworking of horror cinema.

who oppresses the people around his remote castle. *Le Nosferat*, another recent attempt to give the vampire an exclusively political ambiance, casts him in the role of a bourgeois Jack the Ripper. But it is doubtful if such overt transmutations can add much to the original's symbolic power, and they have certainly not revived the subject's popular appeal.

In the meantime it seems that much of the vampire cinema has come to an end. Christopher Lee is adamant that he will not play Dracula again, and no-one has made anything of the part since he renounced it. Even the sex vampire movie has become a declining aspect of the exploitation market. The field will always retain a certain popularity, but what is curious in retrospect is that it should have enjoyed such a specific boom during the late fifties and sixties. Just as Stoker's *Dracula* achieved its vogue in the declining years of Victorian England, the vampire cinema seems itself to have reflected a transitional period in western culture, involving especially the further weakening of traditional sexual morality.

This relationship was only possible because the cinema remains the most effective reproduction of the dream experience that has yet been devized. The psychoanalyst Kurt Lewin was so impressed with the resemblance between the two that he postulated a kind of 'dream-screen' on which our dreams are projected while we sleep. According to his schema, the cinema screen is simply a therapeutic recreation of our own internal screens. So if the vampire has begun to leave the cinema, it is because he no longer plays inside our own heads, and has ceased to be a part of western civilization's dreams and nightmares.

However, it should be remembered that the Dracula mythos, like the villain from whom it derives, has shown a historical tenacity that is too easily underestimated. In Van Helsing's words: 'He may not enter anywhere at first, unless there be some one of the household who bid him to come . . . afterwards he can come as he please.' He has abandoned our dreams now. It is fascinating to speculate on the cultural circumstances which might permit him to re-enter them.

INDEX

Figures in italics refer to illustrations

FURTHER READING

A number of very detailed filmographies of vampire films have appeared recently, notably in *The Seal of Dracula* by Barrie Pattison, in *Photon* 19 and 20 and in *L'Ecran Fantastique*, series 2, numbers 2 and 5. The following titles are also relevant to the history of vampire lore and its attendant psychology and the vampire film:

Beck, Calvin Thomas: *Heroes of the Horrors*, Collier, 1975

Brosnan, John: *The Horror People*, Macdonald and Jane's, 1976

Jones, Ernest: *On the Nightmare*, Liveright, 1951

Lee, Walt: *Reference Guide to Fantastic Films*, Chelsea-Lee Books, 1974

Ludlam, Harry: *Biography of Dracula, the Life Story of Bram Stoker*, Foulsham, 1962

Pattison, Barrie: *The Seal of Dracula*, Lorrimer (UK) and Bounty Books (US), 1975

Pirie, David: *A Heritage of Horror*, Gordon Fraser, 1973

Ronay, Gabriel: *The Dracula Myth*, W. H. Allen, 1972

Silver, Alan and Ursini, James: *The Vampire Film*, Barnes, 1976

Stoller, Robert J.: *Perversion, the Erotic Form of Hatred*, The Harvester Press, 1976

Todorov, Tzvetan, *A Structural Approach to a Literary Genre*, Case Western Reserve University Press, 1973

Wolf, Leonard: *A Dream of Dracula*, Popular Library, 1972

ACKNOWLEDGEMENTS

The author wishes to thank Sherry Zeffert for expert assistance with the manuscript, Tom Walmsley for recommending the work of Robert Stoller, David and Barbara Stone for showing him the Cinegate print of *Vampyr*, and Jimmy Carreras and Chris Wicking of Hammer and, especially, Jude. The publisher wishes to extend very special thanks to Frédéric Lévy and Jean Rollin for their unflagging assistance in providing illustrations for this book. Thanks is also due to the following individuals and organizations for their help in providing illustrations: Anthony Burton, Joel Finler, Colin Maher, Barrie Pattison, Fred Zentner of the Cinema Bookshop London, American International Pictures, Anglo-Amalgamated Film Distributors, Cinegate, EMI Film Distributors, Fox-Rank Distributors, Gaumont-International, Hammer Films, Iduna Film Munich, Lotus Films Madrid, MGM-EMI Distributors, MGM Inc, Monarch Film Corporation, National Film Archive London, Paramount Pictures, Rank Organisation, Universal-International, Warner Bros. Inc, Warner-Columbia Distributors and Warner-Pathé Distributors. Copyright in the illustrations is the property of the production or distribution companies concerned.